CASCADIA
GARDENING
SERIES

Winter
Ornamentals

For the Maritime Northwest Gardener

Daniel J. Hinkley

Sasquatch Books
Seattle

To my parents, Ralph Kirkland Hinkley and Vivian Clara Yunk Hinkley,
who found time to expose their children to the marvels of nature,
from which I have developed my lifelong interest in plants.

Series editor: Jan Silver
Manuscript editor: Alice Copp Smith
Cover design: Kris Morgan Design
Interior design: Lynne Faulk Design
Composition: grafX

Photographs in color insert: Art Dome: p.4, bottom. Daniel Hinkley: p.1, top
and bottom right; p.6, middle left and bottom right; p.8, top, middle, and
bottom left. David McDonald: p.1, middle left, bottom left, top right; p.2,
all; p.3, top and bottom; p.4, top right; p.5, all; p.7, middle and bottom; p.8,
top right and bottom right. Natureview Photos: p.3, middle; p.4, middle left;
p.6, top; p.7, top.

Cover photograph: *Callicarpa bodinieri* var. *giraldii* 'Profusion'
provides a display of rich lavender berries in early winter.
Photograph by Joy Spurr, Natureview Photos.

Library of Congress Cataloging in Publication Data
Hinkley, Daniel J.
    Winter Ornamentals / Daniel J. Hinkley.
        p.   cm. — (Cascadia gardening series)
    Includes bibliographical references (p.) and index.
    ISBN 0-912365-87-0 : $8.95
        1. Winter gardening—Northwest Coast of North America. 2. Plants,
Ornamental—Northwest Coast of North America. I. Title. II. Series.
    SB439.5.H56 1993
    635.9'53— dc20   93-26804
                                                                          CIP

Published by Sasquatch Books
1008 Western Avenue, Suite 300
Seattle, Washington 98104
(206) 441-5555

Other titles in the Cascadia Gardening Series:
Water-Wise Vegetables, by Steve Solomon
North Coast Roses, by Rhonda Massingham Hart
Herb Grower's Handbook, by Mary Preus (forthcoming)

Contents

Acknowledgments   *iv*

Foreword by Rosemary Verey   *v*

Introduction: Northwest Winter Gardening   *vii*

1   Personalizing Your Design   *1*

2   Gardening Basics   *5*

3   Coats of Many Colors: Bark   *10*

4   Enduring Tapestries: Foliage   *22*

5   Blossoms of Winter: Flowers   *37*

6   Colorful Cornucopia: Berries   *62*

    Appendixes
        Plant Characteristics *(Tables)*   *74*
        Public Winter Gardens   *94*
        Plant Buying Directory   *96*
        Bibliography   *98*
        Index   *101*

Acknowledgments

I gratefully acknowledge the many friends and professionals who have instilled in me an appreciation for better plants and planting and have assisted in my odyssey toward conveying this interest to a wider audience: Walt Bubelis, Jerry Flintoff, Toni Haun, Tim Hohn, Arthur Lee Jacobson, Alan Lacy, Roy Lancaster, Steve Lorton, Virginia Morell, Brian Mulligan, Eric Nelson, Jeanne Scholmeyer, Duane West, and John Wott. Thanks to Sarah Reichard for reviewing taxonomic spellings, and to the Elisabeth C. Miller Library of the University of Washington Center for Urban Horticulture for assistance. Special thanks go to Gary Koller, J. C. Raulston, Gerald Straley, and Barry Yinger, who have been both inspirational and supportive of my efforts.

For our winter walks together, as well as for sensitive and intelligent writing that serves as a standard for horticultural writers throughout the world, I wish to thank Rosemary Verey. And, most important, thanks to my friend and partner, Robert Llewellyn Jones, whose support and unselfish dedication to my fanaticism has provided me wings in a world where too often passions are pinioned before the first flight.

Foreword

Special winter days in the Pacific Northwest stand out clearly in my memory. One was spent with Daniel Hinkley, another with David Tarrant at the University of British Columbia Botanical Garden in Vancouver, another with Erica Dunn at the VanDusen Garden, all these on February days. When I drove with Steve Lorton of *Sunset* magazine from Seattle to Vancouver through the Skagit Valley, I was aware of the drama of the evergreen trees clothing the hills and lining the roadsides. My education for appreciating the garden in winter was expanding.

My day with Dan Hinkley, at the Bloedel Reserve and in his own garden in Kingston, was like the pages of a book unfolding—it could have been this book. The sun shone, the air was crisp, and we saw treasure after treasure. There were leaves, berries, colored bark, scented flowers; all the time we were finding nature's ravishing vignettes. You must always see as well as look, or beauty will pass you by. The bark of the maples, the birch and the willows, the red- and yellow-twig dogwoods were sometimes enhanced by dark evergreens, sometimes silhouetted against the sky. Corylopsis in flower was underplanted with hellebores, mingling with the scent of the *Sarcococca hookeriana* 'Purple Stem' nearby.

I picked up and put in my pocket some fallen berries from the yellow holly, *Ilex* 'Bacciflava'. I noticed too the deciduous holly, *I. verticillata*—this has been a favorite of mine since I saw it in its full glory in Bill Frederick's garden in Delaware.

In Dan's own garden and nursery at Heronswood, I was looking for outstanding winter foliage. The conifers, as Dan says, "provide the basic palette of our winter garden," and his chosen *Chamaecyparis lawsoniana* 'Pembury Blue' and C. 'Oregon Blue' are graceful with their dropping branches. I was pleased to see C. 'Lutea' and 'Stewartii', as we have them in our garden in England. The broad-leaved evergreens are just as important for winter interest, and *Berberis stenophylla* × 'Corallina', with its coral red buds opening to yellow and only reaching 3 feet, is ideal for a small garden or a mixed border. I was impressed with the number of different hypericums, rubus, and ribes in Dan's garden, all making a worthwhile contribution.

On my first visit to the University of British Columbia Botanical Garden in Vancouver with David Tarrant, there had just been a fall of snow. We made the only footprints, there was no wind, and the snow was weighing down the branches of the majestic hemlocks and firs. *Clematis orientalis* had clambered through a callicarpa and flakes were still balancing on the berries and the clematis seed heads. The cinnamon-colored bark of a madrona stood out against the whitened landscape. The drooping flowers of *Stachyurus praecox* were familiar to me, but I had never previously seen the soft orange cluster of the blossoms on the evergreen *Sycopsis sinensis*. Another excitement was the flowers of iris, crocus, and chionodoxas pushing through the snow where the covering was lighter. Two Februaries later, when I was in this same garden, the scene was quite different, and as well as walking in the woodland, we were able to thread our way along the narrow paths of the special winter garden. Everything was just as beautiful but this time the pattern of the planting showed up more clearly.

I have long believed that by thoughtful planting we should make autumn join hands with spring in our gardens. The winter months are as important to me as any in the year—I may be enjoying the garden from my windows, noticing the changing light, the shadows, the tracery of trees and shrubs and the precious moments when the sun entices me to walk outside.

I have appreciated my friendship with Dan—our encounters in America and England and our garden visits together have enhanced my winter repertoire. He is a brilliant lecturer, and combines in a refreshing way the scholarship of a botanist and the detailed appreciation of a true gardener. I know that readers of this book will be inspired to observe, plant, and enjoy, and to succeed in making winter a season in its own right. In Dan's words, "Careful observation of colors and textures in the garden will make apparent your own personal slices of the rainbow."

— *Rosemary Verey*

Northwest Winter Gardening

Gardening throughout much of North America is delineated by the four seasons. Landscapes that flourish during the summer are absorbed by the earth in autumn. Along with their creators, they surrender to the torpor of winter until spring reasserts itself.

Even here in the maritime Pacific Northwest, gardening is often rooted in seasonal bias. Until recently, most of the plants available to Northwesterners lent their ornament only to months thought of as the high season of gardening—flashy rhododendrons in the spring, short-lived annuals for summer color, and deciduous trees whose vivid autumnal foliage is extinguished by the first winter rains. Too often our typical winter gardens display little else than the standard conifers, camellias, and pieris.

The garden that brings year-round interest, however, does not ignore the four months of dormancy in our region. Fortunately, during Northwest winters we can continue that most enjoyable and therapeutic activity—gardening. In fact, few parts of North America are as amenable to winter gardening as the northwestern Pacific coast. The western slopes and islands extending from British Columbia to central California are bathed by moderating Pacific currents, resulting in relatively mild winters that provide a rich fourth season of horticultural pleasure.

One of the greatest challenges to a creative designer and plant enthusiast in the Pacific Northwest, then, is to rethink the garden as a twelve-month continuum rather than a seasonal event. In this book, I have assembled a palette of plants whose cycle of colors will help you seamlessly link the four seasons in your landscape. By selecting carefully, you can have a distinct blend of plants for each season, and your landscape will provide interest in form or foliage throughout the year.

Some plants could be repeat performers, while others might offer a solo performance at the zenith of summer or in the depths of winter.

The first two chapters of this book suggest how to analyze your site and improve its soil; how to select species; how to develop your garden design; and finally, how, when, and where to site the plants so that each will thrive. The next four chapters—constituting the majority of the book—introduce choice and unusual plants that can offer interest in our maritime Northwest landscapes from late autumn through early spring. Each of these four chapters addresses a particular ornamental element in the winter garden: bark, foliage, flowers, and berries. Within each chapter you will find trees, shrubs, vines, and perennials that deserve more attention. The tables following Chapter 6 outline specific plant characteristics and requirements, and are designed to assist in the selection of the best plants for your garden.

Although I emphasize the performance of each plant in the winter garden, I also explore its ornamental uses from season to season. For example, I will introduce you to plants that can provide not only beautiful bark in winter but flowers in spring, berries in summer, and leaf color in autumn. Throughout the text, you will also find ways to use these plants as a single focus or as an integral element in borders or foundation plantings. In addition to giving notes on plant culture, I suggest compatible plants that provide pleasing groupings and help span the seasons in your year-round garden.

The quiet, subtle beauty of bark, foliage, flower, and berry can grant unexpected off-season pleasures in spaces that are saturated with splendor during the feverish peak of the gardening cycle. Long after the fray of late spring and early summer, these winter ornamentals will delight the eye and soothe the spirit, from autumn's end to the first days of spring.

—Daniel J. Hinkley

CHAPTER 1

Personalizing Your Design

THE ONGOING GARDEN PROCESS

Some years ago I set about creating my current garden, on the northern end of the Kitsap Peninsula in Washington State's Puget Sound country. Eager to achieve the quick gratification of overflowing perennial borders, I ignored the consequence—a dull and lifeless winter landscape.

Five years later, I rectified my mistake. Because I observe this part of the garden from the living quarters of the house, I had become increasingly unwilling to settle for a flattened, bare landscape from autumn to spring, with nothing to reward the eye. I relegated the herbaceous perennial borders to less prominent positions and converted the original beds into mixed borders that span the seasons. By integrating carefully chosen trees, shrubs, and perennials, I am now beginning to enjoy a garden view that is of interest twelve months a year.

Despite my constant adjustments, though, as long as I am a gardener my garden will never be complete. The true garden design must be thought of in terms not of months but of years. Few good gardens, great or small, would boast of little change during their journey to maturity.

WINTER PLANT SELECTION

Although Northwesterners may be blessed with an environment hospitable to an extraordinary number of fine garden plants, the principles of creating a garden for year-round interest are the same no matter how devilish or benign the prevailing weather.

Begin with a careful study of those plants that you are considering as part of the ultimate design. Only by observing them throughout the year will you be able to develop an appreciation for their performance in every season. Keep a running list of plants that you want to include by gleaning them from books, articles, and lectures. Visit nurseries and

1

public or private gardens during the off season, notebook in hand. (See "Public Winter Gardens" in the back of this book for a selected list.) Even if you employ a garden designer to plan and/or install your garden, take an active role in deciding what plants are to be included. Your designer will appreciate your interest, and the finished product will more closely match your initial expectations.

Not all gardening sites are created equal, however, and experience is the best instructor. Experiment with a multitude of plants, and then retain the best performers. Ultimately, you will be more satisfied with the results. The essence of the design process lies in carefully monitoring your responses to the garden and observing the reaction of garden plants to the environment.

SITE ANALYSIS

Design the garden for year-round interest by first allotting time, during winter, to contemplate the space as it already exists. Annual and perennial beds will be barren, and the ground will be exposed. Deciduous trees and shrubs on or adjacent to your property will no longer be lending their verdant background.

During this time, you can best observe the woody plants that compose the garden's bones and plan to arrange them to add strength and substance throughout the year. Additionally, your resolve to create a garden with a longer period of enjoyment will be at its strongest, undistracted by summer flowers and foliage. The emptiness or dreariness of your garden after leaf fall will be fully exposed. What you observe during this first winter of planning is the naked truth that will affect your future garden design during the winter third of the calendar.

PLANT PLACEMENT

After observing the space and beginning acquisition of plants, you must make decisions about the arrangement and placement of plants in the garden. The beginning gardener can relax with the realization that few landscaping decisions are cast in concrete. In general, if a plant doesn't work in a particular location, you can move it.

Once, while skiing a frightfully steep slope, I overheard an instructor tell his student to ski the mountain 5 feet at a time, rather than tackling the fear of the entire run. I apply this wisdom to the design of the garden. Although it is important to have an overall scheme, the approach to plant placement begins with a design nucleus for each bed. This nucleus can consist of one plant, or it can be a pleasing combination of two or more plants. From here I continue the theme outward, until it eventually meets and unifies with an adjoining theme.

Repeatedly ask yourself several questions as you compose small pictures, each of which will become part of a larger portrait. Will the ratio of evergreen to deciduous ground covers, shrubs, and trees be balanced throughout the year? Is there room to incorporate perennials, annuals, and bulbs for spring and summer effect? At what time of year will each plant provide the best effect, and will there be plants of interest during each season? Do the plants provide a variety of textures for the garden? Will the colors complement or contrast with adjacent colors? Are there fragrant plants throughout the winter, and are they placed where they can be enjoyed?

Current rules of planting insist on sweeps of plants in our gardens, instead of a freckled frenzy of different species. Indeed, plants often have more punch in any garden when used in mass rather than individually. Some gardens have drifts so massive, however, that viewers must stand several feet from the border to observe any communication between one group of plants and their neighbors. Instead, the scope of the massing should be in relation to the size of the space. A grouping of three red-twig dogwoods in a small urban landscape, for example, can produce the same effect as a mass of thirty in a large estate garden. Although I admire and respect gardeners who can use plants as the medium in brilliant design, my deepest regard is reserved for people who simply enjoy plants as nouns, rather than as utilitarian adjectives.

Planning for Fragrance

Adding depth and dimension to the winter garden by including fragrant plants awakens your senses to more than color alone. Indeed, many of the most fragrant winter-blossoming plants have flowers that are a bit on the disappointing side in appearance. Site the most fragrant plants in locations you most often pass during the dour depths of winter—along the walkway to the main entrance, near the garage, or next to the driveway.

Working with Color

Contrasting and complementing hues and tones provide a solidifying influence on garden design. To the uninitiated, principles and dogmas associated with color often seem abstruse and forbidding. Nonetheless, experiment by trial and error, and witness how cohesive a good color scheme can be.

I once walked with a well-known British gardener and author through his magnificent garden in southeastern England's county of Kent. He led me to a specimen of *Spiraea* × *bumalda* 'Goldflame', brightly clad in fresh orange-red foliage maturing to burnished gold. Bright blue and pink hyacinths underplanted the pyrotechnics.

"How do you like my combination?" my host asked. With the frankness that was expected of me, I admitted that I did not. "Not many people do," my host chuckled contentedly, "but I love it."

This underscores the need to follow your own sense of proper color combinations. The bottom line is personal satisfaction with the end result. Although many of the principles of visual art do indeed hold true in horticulture, careful observation of colors and textures in the garden will make apparent your own personal slice of the rainbow.

CHAPTER 2

Gardening Basics

SOIL DEVELOPMENT

Most homes nowadays are built by scraping and hauling away the native topsoil and backfilling with compacted subsoil, resulting in a tilth comparable to that of frozen cookie dough. Although you may never recreate the depth of good soil that your property originally possessed, with moderate effort and cost you can come close. It is hard to spend money on something that seemingly adds no real adornment, but it is important to consider and value the earthy component of your landscape. By improving your soil conditions, you will be amply repaid in the ultimate health and vigor of your garden. Clay or sandy soils will benefit from any organic amendment, such as manure, peat moss, fine bark, compost, sawdust, or commercial topsoil.

In my garden, I developed each of my beds with various types of organic matter—depending upon their availability at the time, and erring on the side of generosity. Four inches of any organic matter, or approximately 10 yards per 1,000 square feet, is the absolute minimum to work into the soil; any less provides little benefit. Ideally, add a total of 8 inches, in two 4-inch increments. Thoroughly mix the first increment with the soil you have inherited, add the second, and mix again.

Certain organic soil amendments, such as sawdust and bark, temporarily rob the soil of nitrogen as the living microbes work to break these components down. Actual nitrogen at a rate of one pound per 1,000 square feet should be integrated into the soil along with sawdust and bark to prevent a nitrogen deficiency from developing in the plants. For example, if you purchase a bag of 20(N)–10(P)–15(K) fertilizer, you have purchased 20 percent actual nitrogen, 10 percent phosphorus, and 15 percent potassium. Therefore, five pounds of this fertilizer must be applied for each 1,000 square feet in order to benefit from one pound of actual nitrogen.

The commercial term "topsoil" is as definitive as the term "soup of the day." I have learned the hard way that it is far less expensive to adjust the soil conditions you have inherited than to remove a costly and structurally defective truckload of sand, clay, or silt that has been dumped on your site. Be absolutely sure you understand what the "top-soil of the month" is before it is delivered.

Another school of thought suggests that amending your soil is simply mulching your garden with dollar bills. Instead, it is proposed, simply grow plants that are suited to your existing soil. Intellectually, I can accept this argument as an intelligent approach to the use of our land—in harmony, rather than in conflict. As a plant collector, however, I rebel at the thought of adhering to the horticultural version of, "When life gives you lemons, make lemonade."

Whatever your approach, take precautions during garden development to preserve whatever resource you have inherited. Most important, do not work the soil when it is too wet. This damages its structure and leads to compaction. During and after bed preparation, walk on it as little as possible. The benefit of richly amended and double-dug beds is lost if the top 6 inches become compacted by foot traffic.

Nearly all soils of the western slope, from British Columbia southward to Northern California, are acidic by nature. Fortunately, the majority of plants that tolerate our climatic conditions also thrive in slightly acidic soils—those with a pH of from 5.5 to 6.5. In discussing the plants in the following chapters, this is the ideal soil I assume you have.

Recently there has been much ballyhoo over the addition of polymers to the soil for increased water-holding potential. There is little evidence that these polymers provide much in the long-term survivability of plants, except in containers. I will avoid their use in the garden until more data can be provided as to what long-term effects these long-lived polymers will have on soil air space and structure.

WHERE TO PLANT

The moderating influence of the Pacific Ocean, which keeps us warmer in the winter, also keeps us cool in summer. Considering our large number of gray days, we find that plants that must be protected from full sun in warmer climates perform admirably in open locations in the maritime Northwest, if provided adequate moisture during the growing season. Occasionally, however, we encounter plants that simply cannot tolerate a full dose of solar radiation and must be given protection, such as *Vinca minor* and species of *Sarcococca*.

In the Northwest, a popular question is "How much shade will this plant tolerate?" A better question would be "What plants can tolerate dry shade?" With the overstory predominance of tall coniferous trees along the West Coast, gardeners most often require plants that like partial or full shade, and that will also compete with the water-greedy root systems of our native flora.

Throughout this book I use the terms "full sun," "partial shade," and "full shade," defined as follows:

Full sun: Direct sunlight for at least six hours a day.
Partial shade: Brightly filtered sunlight for at least six hours a day, or direct sunlight for less than six hours.
Full shade: Heavily filtered but bright conditions, with no direct sun.

WHEN TO PLANT

Containerized plants can be put in the ground at any time of the year. However, avoid trying to establish a plant before or during hard winter freezes. Bare-root trees and shrubs are sold only during early spring, and would suffer, for obvious reasons, if transported and planted during the growing season.

The benefits of autumn planting should be more frequently emphasized by American horticultural literature. Europeans have long understood the advantages of planting their trees, shrubs, and perennials in the fall. Although plants seem quite dormant above ground at this time of the year, most of their root systems are abuzz with activity in the fall. An autumn-planted specimen will make much more growth during the subsequent spring than will its spring-planted equivalent.

HOW TO PLANT

If the root ball is solid and matted, it is extremely important to score this root mass well before you plant. With a sharp knife, make no fewer than four vertical cuts to 1 inch in depth along the entire length of the root ball. Additionally, cut an X into the bottom. This technique helps prevent the development of a girdling root system and encourages more rapid root establishment. Inspect bare-root trees for damage or potential girdling roots, and prune before planting, keeping the roots moist during the process. Wide, saucerlike planting holes, instead of deep, narrow holes, will accommodate the new root system of most plants that grow within the top 6 inches of topsoil.

Mix a handful of superphosphate fertilizer into the soil at the bottom of the planting hole to create an environment that is beneficial for root development; our native soils tend to be deficient in this element. A balanced fertilizer with phosphate is also acceptable. After planting, backfill the hole with the soil you removed when digging it. Resist the temptation to backfill with rich topsoils or amendments. Your benevolence will actually impede the ultimate development of root systems because they will want to stay put within their luxurious confines.

Immediately after planting, water thoroughly, even if rain is forecast. More plants are lost due to insufficient irrigation immediately after planting than for any other reason. Once you have watered them deeply, leave the plants to your regular irrigation practices.

WATER REQUIREMENTS

Our obsession with water-wise planting in the maritime Northwest is enigmatic to the visitor, who envisions this region as a land of ubiquitous drizzle. Our winter wet/summer dry climate comes as a surprise to all but those who have experienced the weeks from mid-June until November with no measurable precipitation. Most plants are adaptable to this condition when fully established. In all but the most severe extended drought, a plant with a well-developed root system can withstand the rigors of extended periods without water.

During establishment, it is better to water deeply and regularly than shallowly and sporadically. This principle applies both to hand watering and to automatic overhead or drip-irrigation systems. Shallow watering (less than 1 inch of water applied) encourages a root system closer to the surface of the soil, thus lessening the ability of trees, shrubs, and perennials to withstand periods without water. To help develop root systems deep enough to endure future years of extended drought, water the soil deeply, to a depth of 12 inches, every other week during the growing season for the first two years of establishment.

INSECTS AND DISEASE

Nearly every plant eventually meets up with an insect or disease partner with which it must share its bounty. Whether introduced or native, plants are generally less susceptible to hosting these living agents if their overall health and vigor has not been compromised. Where it is appropriate, I will note those plants that are generally associated with any particular predator—fungi, bacteria, or insect.

I adhere to the concepts of Integrated Pest Management, and use a variety of a pest control strategies (cultural, mechanical, biological, and chemical). I strongly recommend that you exhaust the first three options, including removal of the plant, before applying pesticides. Resort to any chemical only after reading the label closely to be sure that it can be applied safely. Remember that the insects feasting on your garden have, in turn, their own predators, which may be equally affected by the pesticide application. Caring for the health of this planet through global action starts in your tiny backyard.

PRUNING

Raise up your shrub or tree with a heavy hand and benevolent wisdom, and you will not spoil the results. Too many gardeners put off pruning until it is unavoidable rather than treating it as a yearly maintenance task. If you follow some simple rules you will seldom, if ever, permanently spoil the plant. In fact, as you gain experience, you will realize that your original attempts were overly timid.

Community college and state extension courses abound on the techniques of controlling, shaping, and rejuvenating trees, shrubs, and vines. A day in the field with an experienced pruner can equal weeks of trying to decipher those annoying, "easy-to-follow" line drawings in pruning manuals.

CHAPTER 3

Coats of Many Colors: Bark

TREES AND SHRUBS

As the last colored leaves drift earthward, varnished with the first winter rains, deciduous trees begin to bare their sinewy musculature. Although they may be admired during the growing season, their bare outlines in a sleeping landscape also provide color, texture, and form to enliven the stark scenes of winter. Too often this epidermal layer receives less attention in the garden than do foliage, flower, and fruit; yet it is the skin of these plants that is with us through the calendar, not their more ephemeral attributes.

Sensually smooth and bronze, brilliantly red or yellow, ghostly white, and patchwork quiltings of red, gray, green, and brown—all of these can describe the coats of many colors provided by the bark of woody plants. Both coniferous and deciduous trees add interest to our landscapes through the infinite diversity of this effect.

Acer (Maple)

Among the aristocrats of trees to include in our gardens are the many and varied species of maples, found in the genus *Acer*. Many maple species are surprisingly stronger in their winter attributes than in their foliage and fruit.

Acer davidii, one of several species referred to as the stripebark or snake-bark maples, is a lovely small understory tree native to China that is best suited to partial shade. Nearly unlobed leaves of dark green turn striking shades of orange to red or soft yellow in autumn, depending upon the individual. Young branches turn red in winter; older wood offers smooth polished bark with vertical etchings of jagged white lines.

Acer rufinerve, the redvein maple from Japan, is another species of stripebark maple that is planted for the effect of its beautiful bark as well as for its autumn leaf color. A distinctive identifying and ornamental characteristic of this species is the blue-white coating laid down on the young branches. As the wood ages, this waxy white fades to expose green and white stripes running vertically along the stems and main trunk.

Another stripebark is **Acer tegmentosum**, the Manchurian striped maple. The large leaves emerge from glaucous twigs with a papery texture and an exuberant shade of green. The autumn color is an early yellow that softens the bright colors of the season. However, its ghostly bare trunk and its branches with finely dissected stripes of green and white are what I most admire in this species. It creates a striking effect among the deep greens and dull browns of quiet winter.

Acer pensylvanicum, from the eastern coast of the United States, is the only stripebark maple to occur natively, outside of East Asia. Nearly identical in appearance to A. *tegmentosum* but more readily available, it boasts very finely dissected white stripes on its branches, without the stark intensity of its Chinese counterpart. **A. pensylvanicum 'Erythrocladum'** takes the striped bark look a step further by intensifying young twigs in nearly fluorescent shades of pink and red.

CULTURE: The stripebark maples thrive in landscapes with a tall overstory of Northwest native conifers. Avoid placing them in full sun, to prevent the beautiful bark from being hideously scorched. Once a tree is established, little or no additional summer water is required.

YEAR-ROUND INTEREST: Unfortunately, the most intense autumn color, in shades of orange and red, is achieved in full-sun situations that often ruin the effects of bark. Consider opting for less autumn color.

PLANT COMBINATIONS: Place in front of dark-foliaged conifers for a remarkable winter scene of white-hot flame, often with an aura of glowing coals from the colorful young twigs. Use these trees for their graceful ghostly, spreading scaffolding that stands elegant in the winter landscape.

Acer griseum, commonly known as the paperbark maple, a small tree (to 30 feet) in cultivation, holds year-round interest from cinnamon-brown peeling bark. During the bleak winter months, however, its beauty is even more greatly appreciated. After years of scarcity in the nursery trade, it is now widely available to the maritime Northwest gardener.

CULTURE: Unlike the stripebark maples, the paperbark maple is tolerant of—and even prefers—full sun. Water requirements are moderate to low once it is established.

YEAR-ROUND INTEREST: The trifoliate leaves turn brilliant shades of red and orange in autumn, if the tree is sited with adequate sunlight.

PLANT COMBINATIONS: The flaky copper-colored bark of this species lends itself to many intriguing uses. Consider planting it with winter-blossoming *Stachyurus praecox*, whose midwinter drooping spikes of yellow flowers on burgundy stems sparkle in contrast to *Acer griseum*'s bark.

Arbutus

On a rainy winter's day, there is no more beautiful sight than the blending of the wet, glossy, cinnamon-colored bark of our native madrona, **Arbutus menziesii**, with the dark greens of the native conifers. Although I hope homeowners will continue to value this species and preserve its current foothold in our urban ecology, we should also consider two hybrids for our landscapes, both of superior garden utility because of their smaller size and greater tolerance for human meddling.

Arbutus 'Marina' is a relative newcomer to cultivation, although it was first selected in 1943. This lovely small tree has a coppery-red coating of branches and trunk. Another hybrid, **A. x andrachnoides**, is remarkable for the colors of its bark—a patchwork of chalk, lime, and bronze.

CULTURE: *Arbutus* species grow naturally in dry sites, lending themselves to drought-tolerant landscape designs. Plant in full sun with sufficient drainage. *A. menziesii* is notoriously untidy throughout the year, so take care to place it where the continual fallout can be tolerated and its eventual large size accommodated.

YEAR-ROUND INTEREST: Enjoy the glossy foliage throughout the year, the large clusters of bell-shaped white (*A. menziesii* and *A. x andrachnoides*) or pink (*A.* 'Marina') flowers in autumn, and the grapelike clusters of gritty orange-red fruit in autumn.

PLANT COMBINATIONS: Members of the Ericaceae family, madronas are culturally and aesthetically compatible with heathers and other plants that resent summer water, such as *Cistus* and *Helianthemum*. The native madrona is striking when skirting a sunny margin of a large stand of native conifers.

Arctostaphylos

Of the many broad-leaved evergreens for the garden, few are as effective in bark as the many species of manzanita, **Arctostaphylos**. Our common ground-covering native, the kinnickinnick, *A. uva-ursi*, is a member of this distinguished group of shrubs, though this species is grown more for its evergreen foliage than for the effects of its bark.

The taller, more erect species are more thoroughly admired during the winter months for the effects of their bark and flowers. *Arctostaphylos canescens*, from Oregon and northern California, is among the finest, with leathery leaves of blue-silver arranged on picturesque, contorted branches of rich, polished mahogany. The common manzanita from California, **A.** *manzanita*, ultimately produces an irregular-shaped small tree or large shrub with darker, smaller, green leaves and similar glossy, bronzed bark that seems too finely finished to be a product of nature. During the snappy, cold mornings of late winter, marvel at the beauty of its dainty drooping clusters of pink-blushed bells produced on the branch tips. Another native Washingtonian, **A.** *columbiana*, is eminently acceptable for smaller gardens, with its grayish green leaves on a rounded shrub and its typical beauty of bark.

CULTURE: Manzanitas are extremely drought-tolerant; they cheerfully accept full sun, heat, and limited water, provided the soil is well drained. Although quite common in the drier sites of western Washington, they are only occasionally encountered in specialty nurseries. Selectively prune to open the inner scaffolding of these shrubs.

YEAR-ROUND INTEREST: The lovely evergreen foliage enhances the garden throughout the year. Elegant, nodding, white-to-pink flowers in dense terminal clusters are produced in late winter or early spring.

PLANT COMBINATIONS: Heaths, heathers, and some rhododendrons, found in the same family, are good plant combinations in the landscape because all require full sun and acidic soil. Also consider sun-lovers such as *Cistus, Ceanothus, Cotinus, Yucca, Lavandula, Santolina,* and *Rhus.*

Betula (Birches)

To overlook **Betula** species (birches) in a chapter devoted to bark is tantamount to ignoring petunias in a discussion of long-blossoming summer annuals. It is not a question of *whether or not* to plant birches but of *where* to place them in the landscape—away from underlying objects that may inherit the sticky rain produced by aphids.

The most lovely and deserving birch to plant is an infrequently encountered Himalayan species, **Betula albo-sinensis var. *septentrionalis***. Satin-smooth pink and silver bands cover the trunk and older branches of this tree, which grows to 50 feet. One of the true delights of being involved in horticultural education is showing this species to students and seeing them marvel at a plant so unjustifiably scarce in the maritime Northwest (although it is becoming more readily available in nurseries).

Common European birches have been usurped by landscape designers, who are currently planting thousands of **Betula jacquemontii**. This Himalayan species dons brilliant and nearly flawless chalky white bark and ultimately reaches 45 to 50 feet in height. It tolerates moderately moist soils.

Tolerant of wet soils is **Betula nigra**, the river birch. Rising to 50 feet or higher, it is one of the finest of the birch species for Northwest gardens. Crisp and papery flakes of coppers and pinks are densely plastered along the trunk. 'Fox River' produces an exceptional dwarf tree, 10 feet by 10 feet, with similar striking bark.

Two shrubby birches worthy of mention are **Betula nana** and **B. apoiensis**. B. nana is a low-sprawling shrub with coppery bark and small dime-sized leaves of green during the summer. It tolerates moist areas but succeeds as well in average garden loam. B. apoiensis deserves greater recognition as a small tree or large shrub that offers polished coppery bark throughout the year. This species tolerates a range of soil types, from quick-draining scree to continually moist situations.

CULTURE: With the beauty of birches come pitfalls and detriments. However, do not avoid planting these trees because of their susceptibility to aphids, which provide an abundance of food to many bird species. Carefully site birches away from main areas of human activity and planting beds to mimimize the problems of honeydew and black sooty mold that are associated with these insects. Aphids largely prefer the European birches; the Asiatic species remain comparatively untouched. Birches that do not tolerate wet soils or excessive moisture should be placed in full sun or on the southern woodland margin.

YEAR-ROUND INTEREST: Autumn foliage turns a rich soft yellow before falling.

PLANT COMBINATIONS: Birches work well in small groves. The white-to-pink bark can be combined with a number of plants to create dazzling scenes. If planting a birch suitable to well-drained soils, consider placing 'Blue Star' junipers at the base; if space allows, use the larger juniper, 'Blue Pfitzer'. In fall, the ruby red color of Disanthus cercidifolius contrasts wonderfully with the bleached vertical columns. During late winter, complement the birch bark with a trio of red dogwoods (see Cornus, below) or Corylopsis sinensis, with its soft yellow flowers.

Cornus (Dogwood)

Cornus kousa is one of the best all-round garden trees in cultivation, with its tiered floral display in late spring and its outstanding autumn color. Horticulturists, however, are only now beginning to realize how striking the bark is on a maturing specimen of this remarkable year-round tree. Platy patches fall away, exposing younger, brightly colored tissue of browns, greens, and yellows. C. *kousa* and its cultivars are commonly found in the nursery trade. All make outstanding multiseasonal trees.

CULTURE: For best effect, plant *Cornus kousa* in full sun, and provide regular, deep summer irrigation. Although it tolerates partial shade, both its autumn coloration and its spring blossoming are more intense under brighter conditions. Fortunately, C. *kousa* resists anthracnose, which plagues both the eastern and western flowering dogwoods.

YEAR-ROUND INTEREST: Show-stopping flowers in June, handsome dark green summer foliage, decorative fruit resembling oversized raspberries, and intense autumn color—this tree has it all.

PLANT COMBINATIONS: Because of its multifaceted personality, use C. *kousa* as a single lawn specimen. Although it easily integrates into a mixed perennial border or as a foundation tree, it stands on its own merits and does not need other plants to carry it through the year.

The red-twig dogwoods in the genus **Cornus** have long been grown for their intensely red or yellow bark in winter, their primary season of interest. C. *alba* **'Elegantissima'** provides twelve months of interest beyond its bright red winter stems by offering gray-green leaves, neatly margined with white, throughout the summer. The bark of C. *alba* **'Kesselringii'** is remarkably dark red, approaching black-purple. During winter, a massing of this shrub combined with the yellow-twig dogwood, C. *stolonifera* **'Flaviramea'**, for contrasting color, is a bold yet refined composition.

The newly introduced yellow-twig dogwood cultivar **Cornus alba 'Silver and Gold'** has bright yellow stems in winter and lovely white, variegated summer leaves. C. *alba* **'Spaethii'** has orange-red stems throughout the year and bright golden summer foliage. C. *alba* **'Kelseyi'** has proven to be a most remarkable dwarf ground cover, creating a striking winter effect when the very fine, upright, 8-inch stems intensify to fiery orange-red.

CULTURE: Cut these shrubby dogwoods to the ground in early spring of every third year to stimulate new growth and intensify winter color. They perform equally well in soggy conditions or in average garden loam. Place in full sun.

YEAR-ROUND INTEREST: Even though their flowers are insignificant, variegated cultivars of the shrubby dogwoods remain one of the most acceptable year-round shrubs for small landscapes.

PLANT COMBINATIONS: The red-stemmed species are set off by blue-foliaged conifers, as well as with the yellow-stemmed dogwood cultivars. *Salix purpurea* 'Nana', a dwarf willow, creates a soft smoky-purple haze that can soften the brightness of both the red- and yellow-twigged dogwoods, while sharing similar conditions. Site the colorful stemmed dogwoods where you can enjoy the brilliance of the sun reflecting from their twigs.

Corylus avellana 'Contorta'

On the north side of my home, in a bed framed by the window of the breakfast nook, I have sited an assemblage of plants to provide entertainment throughout the seasons. The corkscrew hazel, **Corylus avellana 'Contorta'**, also known as "Harry Lauder's walking stick," is planted here. After leaf drop, the silhouette of its corkscrewed dance becomes apparent in the long spiraled branches.

CULTURE: Place in full sun to partial shade. After the third year, the plant needs no additional summer watering. Grafted specimens often sucker from the noncontorted rootstock, so prune out the "normal" branches regularly. Selectively remove congestion that may result from too many branches to allow fuller enjoyment of the chaotic silhouette.

YEAR-ROUND INTEREST: In late winter, an additional bonus of long, drooping, golden catkins is produced along the branches. These waver in the slightest breeze and, if the sun is angled correctly, the gardener sees a cloud of gold-dusted pollen drifting from the mother ship in an odyssey to pollination. The overall summer effect of this shrub is one of contorted ailment, although the dense and crinkled dark green leaves fortunately seem to disappear if the shrub is planted amidst a colorful summer perennial border.

PLANT COMBINATIONS: Avoid siting against a dark backdrop to best admire the effect of this shrub's contortion. Instead place a lighter-foliaged conifer or broad-leaved evergreen, against which the spiraled stems of this plant will be etched.

Lagerstroemia (Crape myrtle)

The crape myrtles, in the genus **Lagerstroemia**, have been grown in the cooler maritime areas for many years, yet our summers infrequently have the length and warmth required to produce flowers. No matter, as the bark brings us a much longer and more substantive season of interest. Many cultivars and hybrids exist, each bringing a different bark effect—crisp, flaky red; mottled greens; or olive and gray. Crape myrtles are small in the maritime Northwest climate, up to 25 feet tall.

CULTURE: Plant in full sun in the warmest possible location to increase the chances of late-summer flowers. Well-drained loamy soil is beneficial, yet once the tree is fully established, extra summer water is unnecessary.

YEAR-ROUND INTEREST: In the Northwest climate, especially after a warm summer, flowers are produced in shades of red, pink, and pure white, depending upon the cultivar. Look for these large clusters on the ends of branches in late August and September.

PLANT COMBINATIONS: Each cultivar presents its own range of bark and flower color. All benefit from a dark background provided by conifers or broad-leaved evergreens, but also consider placing crape myrtles close to a garden path or walkway to be admired at close range.

Metasequoia glyptostroboides (Dawn redwood)

For extremely wet sites, even areas that flood periodically, consider a tree once known only through fossil evidence. **Metasequoia glyptostroboides**, the dawn redwood, was rediscovered in a remote Chinese valley during World War II. This remarkable tree is among a handful of conifer species worldwide that lose their foliage during the winter months. I most admire its extraordinary cavernous and sinewy, swollen reddish brown trunk. The growth beneath each lateral branch slows in relation to adjacent tissue, resulting in conspicuous rounded pits that become larger and deeper with age. A 30-year-old specimen looks more like an eroded stalagmite than a living plant. Give this tree adequate summer moisture for faster growth, and consider it only if you have enough space to handle an ultimately 75-foot-tall specimen.

CULTURE: This distinctive wet-site plant will even tolerate seasonal standing water. Place in full sun or partial shade. Although it is tolerant of average garden loam, provide additional summer water during its formative years in loamy soil.

YEAR-ROUND INTEREST: Deep green, ferny foliage during the summer months gives way to an autumn display of burnished orange before leaf drop. Thimble-sized cones are produced on older specimens only.

PLANT COMBINATIONS: Site in groves, if space allows. Combined with other lovers of wet soil, such as willows, dogwoods, and *Ilex verticillata*, this tree becomes the focal point in any location.

Parrotia persica (Persian ironwood)

Parrotia persica, the Persian ironwood, grows to 35 feet. It is often thought of as a small tree or large multistemmed shrub whose main offering of ornament is autumn coloration of intense oranges and reds. As the plant matures, however, this witch-hazel relative also develops beautifully mottled bark in flaking patches of green, gray, and brown.

CULTURE: Plant in full sun so *Parrotia* can develop its finest coloration. Refrain from trying to force it as a single-stemmed tree; otherwise, much of its grace will be lost, and you will have the continual chore of removing basal suckers. It is extremely drought-tolerant once established.

YEAR-ROUND INTEREST: After the striking oranges and reds of autumn, find small winter flowers borne along the stems, similar in appearance to those of the witch hazels. Individually, the red flowers are insignificant; collectively, they produce a rusty red cloud of subtle beauty.

PLANT COMBINATIONS: Keep an open background to allow fuller enjoyment of the rather small winter flowers. *Parrotia* contrasts beautifully in a group planting with birches and smaller dark green conifers.

Persea yunnanensis

Persea yunnanensis (= *P. ichangense*), a hardy member of the genus that brings us the culinary avocado, is an outstanding tree with distinctive foliage that is linear and glossy. Perhaps its best ornamental trait is its highly textured black skin, reminiscent of tanned alligator hide. Dark textural columns of swarthy bark create a dramatic scene when planted in small groves.

CULTURE: This species forms a columnar tree to 35 feet. No additional summer water is required after it is well established. Extremely cold winters result in leaf burn if the tree is exposed to drying winds.

YEAR-ROUND INTEREST: The handsome evergreen leaves are nearly six times longer than they are wide.

PLANT COMBINATIONS: Place under Northwest native conifers or on the woodland margin in a site that will maximize light while providing the moderating influence of the overstory. Although you must wait several years to admire the bark effect of this tree, you can create a dazzling scene by underplanting it with the white-stemmed species of *Rubus*, such as *R. cockburnianus.*

Pinus (Pine)

Many **Pinus** species are known for lovely platy bark, but the best of the lot may be **Pinus bungeana**. Although you must wait for the effect—and the wait could be some time, indeed—the bark develops into a dazzling patchwork of white, gray, brown, and green as the plant matures. Few plants rival this pine for bark effect alone. Often found in temple gardens in its native China, this species has recently become more widely available in the Pacific Northwest. If you lack the patience for a 20-year wait, substitute the Japanese red pine, **P. densiflora**, which quickly develops a warm, reddish, and elegantly irregular trunk.

CULTURE: Plant in full sun, in well-drained soil. Supplemental summer water will increase its growth rate from agonizingly slow to very slow. The best fertilizer to use is patience, as you wait for the bark effects to develop.

YEAR-ROUND INTEREST: Medium green needles in bundles of three are loosely held on the crown of this narrowly upright tree.

PLANT COMBINATIONS: Use in a foundation planting without the risk of its outgrowing its location. As the bark effects develop, selectively remove branches to expose the colorful trunk, or instruct your heirs to do so.

Pseudocydonia sinensis

Pseudocydonia sinensis, native to China, is a rare relative of the quince. I first encountered this species while in Japan, and marveled at its intensely beautiful bark, which takes on shades of white, gray, green, and brown. Later I discovered that several specimens are thriving throughout the Northwest in public gardens. This outstanding multi-seasonal small tree deserves more attention by horticulturists.

CULTURE: Plant in full sun and well-drained soil, allowing space for a round-crowned tree to 25 feet tall and 20 feet wide.

YEAR-ROUND INTEREST: Pink apple blossom–like flowers are produced in early spring, followed by very large oblong fruits that are hard as rocks even when ripe. Specimens growing in full sun display autumn tints of red and pink.

PLANT COMBINATIONS: A gnarled specimen of this species, in full sun, would easily accept a rose climbing into its branches, providing a striking arbor of highly textural and colorful wood. Select a less-vigorous climber for this effect, such as the repeat performer 'New Dawn', which has fragrant, double peachy pink blossoms.

Salix (Willow)

The many species of willow, genus **Salix**, surpass the diversity of character claimed by the shrubby dogwoods, yet share their ability to tolerate a wide range of soil types. Several willow species, among them **S. gracilistyla** and **S. daphnoides**, have a lovely chalky bloom on their branches, which becomes more apparent during the winter months. Young whitish branches provide striking effect in the winter, rising upright to the sky like narrow jets of white smoke. These species can produce sizable trees over time, to 40 feet if not restricted by regular coppicing.

Salix purpurea 'Nana' is wonderful for bluish green summer foliage as well as winter bark. Upon leaf drop in autumn, the smoky purple stems are exposed, revealing a subtle beauty that remains effective throughout the winter. This well-behaved shrub remains less than 6 feet tall and seldom needs pruning. Although it thrives in the moist soils of our pond edge, it will flourish in ordinary garden soil when given occasional supplemental water.

Few shrubs can compete with the brilliance in bark effect of two varieties of *Salix alba*, the white willow. *S. alba* var. *vitellina*, the goldtwig willow, has stems of striking egg-yolk yellow; the color intensifies when the shrub is severely pruned yearly. The stems of *S. alba* 'Britzensis' flare intensely orange-red during winter months.

CULTURE: As the bark becomes less attractive on older wood, willows grown for bark effect must be coppiced regularly. Cut each branch back to its base in early spring to increase the number of young branches produced and to control the ultimate size. Although best grown in full sun with moist soils, willows surprisingly tolerate a great deal of drought if established in standard garden soil.

YEAR-ROUND INTEREST: Like mercurial droplets along the stem, catkins in late winter or spring shimmer in silver when lit by the winter sun. Many willows can be grown for their winter flowers alone, including *Salix melanostachys*, with its jet black catkins and red anthers, as well as *S. chaenomeloides*, which produces enormous and lovely catkins of silvery white to 3 inches in length.

PLANT COMBINATIONS: For winter interest, integrate willows with other shrubs that have complementing colors and features or that provide a background for bark. Because they tolerate wet soils, willows are in perfect accord with the red- and yellow-stemmed dogwoods for contrast of color and texture. The many species of willows are so diverse in appearance that they can easily be combined in the landscape without fear of monotony.

Stewartia

The genus **Stewartia** is a small but exceptional group of plants closely allied to camellias. The commonly available **S. pseudocamellia** is the coarser-textured of the two Asiatic species frequently put to use. During winter, a sturdy framework of branches becomes chiseled with colorful patches of bark in rusts, greens, and grays. This exceptional anchoring component for our gardens ultimately produces a sizable specimen, to 40 feet or more, in the maritime Northwest climate.

A more finely textured effect of crisp cinnamon is found on a maturing specimen of **Stewartia monodelpha**. S. koreana, sometimes encountered in local nurseries, is the Korean counterpart of Japan's S. pseudocamellia and is very similar in appearance.

CULTURE: Place in full sun or partial shade for best autumn color, although shady conditions are more beneficial to the bark. Leaf scorch occurs if the tree is not given adequate water during its first years of establishment. Lessen supplemental summer water as it matures. These carefree plants require little attention beyond simple appreciation of their beauty.

YEAR-ROUND INTEREST: A sensational display of delicate white camellia-like flowers emerges from satiny buds in late spring. Place in full sun or light shade for a long-lasting autumn symphony of reds, oranges, and burgundy.

PLANT COMBINATIONS: Place where the bark can be admired throughout the winter season. Ideally, integrate within the mixed border, or for height in foundation beds.

CHAPTER 4

Enduring Tapestries: Foliage

Flowers and fragrance dazzle our senses, and the fruits of autumn and winter are jewels to be coveted, yet the seasons of these attributes are ephemeral. Foliage is the ornament longest appreciated by the gardener.

The needles of conifers, as well as the leaves of broad-leaved evergreens, provide year-round substance to the garden. Strong leaf characteristics best define the garden, and produce a landscape that is rich in interest throughout the calendar. Evergreen shrubs and trees alone do not have a monopoly on winter foliage effects; many ground-covering herbaceous plants also hold their leaves during the winter.

Such plants can carry a garden through the months of dormancy by providing not only foliage but distinctive silhouettes and beautiful bark. However, the incredible foliar variability within the plant kingdom makes literally thousands of distinct forms, sizes, and colors available for our use.

The list of remarkable selections in a range of colors is immense, limited only by the average garden's ability to accommodate the ultimate size of many species and cultivars. As you select plants, include those that provide more than one season of interest.

CONIFERS

Those living in the coniferous center of the universe—the Pacific Northwest—need no reminding that evergreens come in both broad-leaved and needled forms. The conifers present a constant effect of foliage throughout the year, which communicates with the components of our summer landscapes as well as providing the basic palette of our winter gardens.

Below, we only begin the odyssey into this remarkable class of plants that thrive in a range of full sun to shade. An initial exploration of the available species makes apparent that within this primitive group are choices for every situation — from background to focal point — in any landscape. These personal favorites provide a spectrum of hues from intense blue, golden to light yellow, and exceptional green foliage. The intense, steely blues provide a soft elegance which soothes, rather than excites, the senses, while providing a superb foil for other garden components. The variations of gold and bright yellows enliven our frequent sullen, overcast days of winter. Green's neutral splendor is a backdrop to the many other colors included in our gardens. Surrounded by green as we are in the Pacific Northwest, we often overlook this addition to our gardens until winter swallows the lushness of the growing season. The many shades of green provided by conifers are unequaled by any other group of plants and are manifested in textures that only the needled evergreens can provide.

Abies procera 'Glauca' adorns our living rooms at Christmas more often than our year-round landscapes. The exceptional blue-needled cultivars of this noble fir offer nearly unparalleled color intensity. Young grafts, if left unstaked, may oftentimes be more content with a life of prostrate laziness than with becoming upright members of the gardening community. Although temporary staking helps this plant establish a leader, you can also exploit its propensity to prostrateness by allowing the steely blue foliage to snake around the garden as a ground cover.

Few conifers exceed the beauty of a true cedar such as *Cedrus atlantica* 'Glauca', whose steely platinum-tipped needles are among the best. It is rare to see a well-planted and maturing specimen of blue Atlas cedar in a Northwest garden. The human psyche being what it is, the gardener is all too often seduced by the beauty of this tree in the nursery and bears it home regardless of the space available in the garden—only to find after a decade or so that he or she is forced to destroy its magnificent architectural form by ruthless pruning. *C. atlantica* 'Glauca Fastigiata' produces a more narrow and upright specimen than the standard blue form but is not as prettily colored.

Chamaecyparis lawsoniana 'Pembury Blue' and *C. lawsoniana* 'Oregon Blue' are outstanding graceful selections of Lawson's cypress, also known as Port Orford cedar, a native of south-central Oregon. Although they perhaps lack the brilliant early-spring frosted blue found on spruces, they make up for this deficiency by the grace of their gently drooping branches. Both reach 50 feet in height, and respond best in full sun with well-drained, moist conditions. Summer water is not required and may cause root rot. 'Spek' produces a narrow, erect column of rich blue to 40 feet, ideal for narrow sites in the landscape.

The golden-foliaged cultivars of **Chamaecyparis lawsoniana**, including **'Lutea'** and **'Stewartii'**, intensify during the colder winter months, when the sunny side of the tree becomes more brightly colored. Observe many specimens of this tree throughout Northwest public gardens and older residential neighborhoods.

Elegant spiraling, tufted, or arching sprays of shiny dark green are found on many cultivars of **Chamaecyparis obtusa**, known collectively as the Hinoki cypress. Hundreds of forms have been selected by the horticulturists in its homeland of Japan, as well as in Europe and North America.

Chamaecyparis obtusa **'Gracilis'**, known as the slender Hinoki cypress, is hardly narrow at all, yet it forms a graceful, tall shrub with upright branches nodding gracefully at the ends. Its dwarf counterpart, **C. obtusa** **'Nana Gracilis'**, reaches 6 feet over a long period, is more acceptable for a smaller garden, and is delightful for the Van Gogh swirlings of its dark green foliage. Nearly all of the innumerable named selections make exceptional additions to foundation beds, rock gardens, or mixed perennial borders. Plant in full sun.

Cryptomeria japonica **'Elegans Aurea'**, the golden version of the standard plume cryptomeria, is likely to become a popular addition to the list of plants that add winter foliage effects to Northwest gardens. Indeed, **C. japonica** **'Elegans'** itself is a remarkable small conifer, with smoky plumed fans of feathery foliage intensifying to russet during the winter months. 'Elegans Aurea' sports identically textured foliage in shades of soft yellow, but is not as big. Both produce small, manageable trees in our Northwest landscapes, to 25 feet in height over as many years. Plant golden versions in partial shade to avoid leaf scorch. Others need full sun.

Ranking among the most beautiful of the blue conifers grown in the maritime Northwest is **Cupressus glabra** **'Pyramidalis'** or **'Blue Pyramid'**, commonly known as the blue Arizona cypress. This native of central Arizona creates a formal, silver-blue, cone-shaped small tree to 25 feet in height. Most successful in well-drained soil conditions, it likes full sun and is considered among the best drought-tolerant conifers for our landscapes.

Among my favorite ground-covering species is **Juniperus squamata** **'Blue Star'**, a small aristocrat among the conifers we can grow.

Slowly maturing to a neat and tidy mound of intense blue foliage 2 feet by 2 feet, this juniper seldom requires pruning or shearing. 'Blue Star' is a dwarf replacement for the beastly large *J. squamata* 'Meyeri' that is commonly found in our older landscapes. Plant in full sun.

Microbiota decussata, Siberian cypress, is a little-known coniferous ground cover, yet it greatly deserves wider inclusion in Northwest gardens. Finely dissected sprays of bright green foliage spread horizontally to 6 feet without attaining more than 18 inches in height. The green spring and summer foliage darkens to a pleasant russet in late autumn and winter, intensified if it is grown in full sun. Remarkably adaptive, it is equally content in full sun or dense shade.

Picea omorika, Serbian spruce, ranks high on my list of all conifers for grace of habit and beauty in foliage. Unlike the Colorado blue spruce, *P. pungens* 'Glauca', it responds admirably to our climate and remains relatively pest-free and handsome throughout the year. The lateral branches of this narrowly upright species, coated in blue-green needles, gently and gracefully sweep downward and then upward. Plant in full sun or partial shade in average to moist soil.

Picea orientalis is one of my favorite spruces for its lush black-green foliage. Plan on a moderate-sized tree, to 35 feet or higher. This species, along with the Serbian spruce, is one of the few spruces that respond favorably to the cooler, moist climate of the maritime Northwest. The finely textured sprays of dense, dark green needles are pest-free. Plant in full sun for optimum health and vigor.

The golden Scotch pine, *Pinus sylvestris* 'Aurea', changes into its golden winter garb after the first frosts of late autumn. When this two-needled species is placed to catch the low-angled rays of sun during a late winter afternoon, it dazzles with bright sulphur yellow foliage. Ultimately a small tree to 25 feet, it ranks among the best as a distinctive and colorful addition to the winter landscape. For best color effect, plant in full sun.

Taxus baccata 'Standishii', the golden version of the Irish yew, ultimately produces a narrow column of yellow-striped foliage that adds a striking point of exclamation to the winter garden. As with many golden variegates, the color tends to be more intense on the southern, sunny side of the plant. Similar to those of the standard green Irish yew, the erect lines of this shrub lend vertical relief to the landscape. It can also be used as a tall and extremely narrow hedge in a formal garden setting.

Thuja plicata 'Zebrina', a golden variant of our native western red cedar, shines throughout the year with its bands of bright yellow etched on sprays of dark green foliage. Although vigorous, it never approaches the towering size of its native green counterpart. Tolerant of perennially moist areas in our landscapes, it performs in either full sun or partial shade.

Broad-leaved Evergreen Trees, Shrubs, and Perennials

The broad-leaved evergreens add a foliar richness to our winter gardens, as well as presenting flowers and fruit throughout other seasons of the year. The currently used inventory of broad-leaved evergreen trees that one can integrate into the landscapes of the maritime Northwest is a bit thin. Broad-leaved evergreen shrubs, however, come in a seemingly endless variation of foliage colors and variegation, textures, and ultimate heights, for nearly every situation.

Berberis (Barberry)

The ancient Greeks' fondness for an imported drug known as lycium, a cure-all potion, resulted in dubbing the plant from which they thought it was derived as "foreign bark" or "barbarian bark." Over time, this name became attached to another genus with which they were confused, now known as **Berberis**, the barberries.

The genus *Berberis* encompasses both evergreen and deciduous species that are among the most valued plants to include in Western gardens for winter interest. Beyond their beauty of flowers and fruit (see Chapters 5 and 6), evergreen barberries are among the richest foliage plants available for garden structure and strength during winter.

Berberis × stenophylla is a cross between *Berberis darwinii* (see Chapter 5, "Flowers") and another South American species, *B. empetrifolia*. Graceful, arching 6-foot canes of small blue-green leaves are covered in late spring with soft yellow flowers. This cross has resulted in many useful selections, including **B. × stenophylla 'Corallina'**, which produces a compact shrub to 3 feet in height that provides highly textural foliage. Jewel-like buds of red open to rich yellow flowers in late spring. **'Corallina Compacta'**, which seldom exceeds 1 foot in height, is an even tighter version, well suited to the winter rock garden.

Impenetrable thickets of heavily armored stems cloaked with lovely dark green foliage are characteristic of **Berberis julianae**. The leaves of this species, though dark green, may develop rich reds and oranges during the winter if in full sun or under drought stress. Eventually reaching 10 to 12 feet tall, it is an effective and hardy hedge and barrier. **B. × gladwynensis 'William Penn'** is similar to B. *julianae* in nearly all respects but ultimately produces a much more compact and tidy shrub 3 feet or less in height—ideal for a tall ground cover or a low informal hedge.

Berberis calliantha is one of my favorite evergreen barberries. Glossy and toothed rich green leaves with a blinding white waxy undercoating are produced on stems to 3 feet. In full sun, this shrub develops a wonderful tinting of reds and oranges during autumn but reverts to shining green the following spring. Originally named by Brian Mulligan, director emeritus of Seattle's Washington Park Arboretum, it is an outstanding and too infrequently encountered small shrub for our gardens.

CULTURE: The evergreen barberries tolerate semishady positions but develop better autumn color in full sun. Although they are forgiving as to soil type, be sure to provide sharp drainage.

YEAR-ROUND INTEREST: Bright yellow or orange flowers, depending on the species, are produced in early to mid-spring. Some are followed by attractive blue-black fruit in mid- to late summer.

PLANT COMBINATIONS: Beyond their utilitarian roles of hedging and security, barberries add sheer beauty in foliage, flower, and fruit. Easily integrate these shrubs into the woodland garden or sunny mixed border to provide structure throughout the year. Arching canes of blue-green foliage of *Berberis* × *stenophylla* are gracefully elegant rising from an expanse of the Northwest native evergreen ground cover *Vancouveria planipetala*.

Elaeagnus

Elaeagnus pungens, commonly known as silverberry, is a handsome, medium-sized evergreen shrub that deserves more recognition by gardeners. The 4-inch leaves are gray-green above; underneath, they are coated by a scaly covering of intense silver, as are the young stems and ripened red fruit, making all appear splattered by a careless application of silver paint. The shrub ultimately reaches 8 feet by 8 feet, although its height is easily controlled by selective pruning.

Elaeagnus × *ebbingii* 'Gilt Edge' ranks, in my estimation, as one of the most outstanding golden-foliaged shrubs available for our use. Bold golden bands of pigment enliven the dull green of this 6-foot specimen and are perfectly combined with the intense silver-white undercoating of the foliage. 'Gilt Edge' occasionally reverts to standard leaf color, so it must be pruned out on a regular basis.

CULTURE: A wonderfully adaptable shrub, *Elaeagnus* responds best to full sun or semishaded conditions but will tolerate dense, dry shade. It is very drought-tolerant even when young, but it will grow more robustly if given supplemental water in its first seasons. Site this plant where you can admire the undersurface of the leaf and enjoy the autumn fragrance.

YEAR-ROUND INTEREST: Red-speckled silver fruit is produced following remarkably fragrant white blossoms, which open in late autumn.

PLANT COMBINATIONS: The yellow variegated forms are beautiful in combination with any blue summer flower or with the intense lavender berries of *Callicarpa*.

Euphorbia amygdaloides var. *robbiae* (Miss Robb's spurge)

Euphorbia amygdaloides var. *robbiae*, known commonly as Miss Robb's spurge, is well suited for planting at the base of golden-leaved shrubs for the contrast of its dark green leaves. This perennial species, seldom recognized as a euphorb by its first-time admirers, forms a tight, dark green mound that achieves a height of 15 inches and spreads slowly to at least 3 feet across. Known for its ability to withstand drought and deep shade, it responds equally in situations of full sun.

CULTURE: Place in full sun or dense shade; this plant takes all conditions in stride. Remove spent flower stems in late spring to preserve the vigor of the mother plant.

YEAR-ROUND INTEREST: Bright chartreuse flowers are produced in late March and last throughout most of May.

PLANT COMBINATIONS: This is an exceedingly easy ground cover for the garden and fills a niche for a handsome and durable foliage plant, lending interest throughout the year.

Eurya japonica (Eurya)

The rich green leaves of **Eurya japonica** place it high on the list of perennial plants in my garden that I value for foliage. It has proven to be an exceptionally hardy little shrub, sustaining little or no damage from the extremely low temperatures and high winds it was exposed to at an early age. In its selection **'Winter Wine'**, the foliage darkens to a rich, shining burgundy from late autumn through winter. Adaptive to both full sun and partial shade, *Eurya* is reasonably drought-tolerant after initial establishment.

CULTURE: Site in full sun or partial shade with supplemental irrigation until fully established.

YEAR-ROUND INTEREST: Unlike the many striking flowers produced by members of the related camellia family, these small, pink-blushed white flowers are on the disappointing side. They are crowded in the leaf axils in early spring. The heady odor is not considered pleasant by some, so place this plant in the garden according to your personal taste.

PLANT COMBINATIONS: Blend into the mixed shrubbery or foundation planting. Like that of camellias, the foliage adds rich dimension during the winter and provides substance and foil in the summer garden.

Ilex (Holly)

The evergreen hollies, **Ilex spp.**, are among the nobility of garden plants that provide interesting foliage and fruit throughout the year. I cannot resist the temptation to list a handful of hollies that I have included in my garden for foliage effect alone.

Ilex aquifolium 'Flavescens' appears as standard fare during the summer months in shades of green, perhaps lighter than that of regular English hollies. During late fall, as the temperatures cool, however, this shrub transforms into a swirl of gold and yellow, which intensifies as winter settles in. **Ilex 'O Spring'** is equally bright, but the golden color is provided by a distinctive pattern on each leaf. The color intensifies during the winter months, yet it also remains colorful during the summer.

Ilex crenata 'Convexa', the convex-leaf Japanese holly, adds distinctive texture from tiny leaves that are turned downward at the margin, on mounds of dark foliage to 2 feet. It is always a handsome addition to the winter landscape.

CULTURE: Plant evergreen hollies in full sun to partial shade. The golden-foliaged cultivars develop their best variegation in full sun, although the intensity of their display is best exhibited by providing a dark background.

YEAR-ROUND INTEREST: Variegated hollies are not necessarily female plants and therefore cannot be counted on to produce fruit for winter interest. *Ilex crenata* produces shiny black fruit in autumn but is grown mostly for its foliage.

PLANT COMBINATIONS: Planted among deeper greens, the golden-foliaged hollies become a beacon enlivening the garden throughout the winter months. Many cultivars of *I. crenata* are ideal for small, informal hedges but can be sheared if a formal hedge is desired.

Lamium maculatum

Lamium maculatum 'White Nancy', a perennial, provides low mats of pewter-colored leaves held throughout the year. By reflecting automobile headlights during winter and summer alike, the leaves almost serve as runway beacons for guests leaving our home after dinner. The wide-spreading mat of foliage, no higher than 8 inches, produces white blossoms in the axils of its leaves in June and July.

CULTURE: Plant in partial to full shade and supply ample moisture during the growing season. Shear the plants to the ground after they blossom to rejuvenate the foliage.

YEAR-ROUND INTEREST: Flowers of white (or pink in some cultivars) bloom in spring and early summer.

PLANT COMBINATIONS: The silver leaves of this ground cover are extremely effective combined with dark green shrubs such as *Sarcococca*, *Ilex*, or camellias.

Leucothoe

Leucothoe fontanesiana, an exceptional broad-leaved evergreen shrub from the mountains of the eastern United States, provides a distinctive leaf texture for the garden. The leathery green leaves are arranged in a single plane along 4-foot stems that gracefully arch to the ground. Though I find the pure and dark green foliage of this species a very acceptable component of the garden in partial to full shade, the variegated selection, **L. *fontanesiana* 'Rainbow'**, is first-rate for winter interest in foliage. Pink and white strokes of color are swirled about the leaves, like an unevenly blended can of paint. This color is intensified and suffused with purple during the winter months, especially under bright conditions, where it must be given more water.

Unlike its East Coast cousin *Leucothoe fontanesiana*, **L. *davisae***, from southern Oregon and California, produces a stiffly upright low-mounded evergreen shrub to 2 feet, with erect floral spikes produced in late spring. Leave it unpruned after flowering, and the swollen seed capsules take on hints of red and pink during the winter months, in contrast to the dark green of the foliage.

CULTURE: Like all of the Ericaceae, species of *Leucothoe* thrive in a peaty soil if ample summer moisture is provided. When fully established, however, it survives without supplemental summer watering.

YEAR-ROUND INTEREST: From the axillary catkins of *Leucothoe fontanesiana*, held throughout the winter months, are produced drooping racemes of white bell-shaped flowers in April. *L. davisiae* produces bright white flowers on upright stems in late spring.

PLANT COMBINATIONS: Consider these species as superb ground-covering shrubs, well suited to combining with the many species of gaultherias and smaller rhododendrons.

Ophiopogon planiscapus 'Nigrescens' (Black lily turf)

Ophiopogon planiscapus 'Nigrescens', a grassy look-alike related to the lily, is a remarkable low-growing ground cover with jet black foliage of incomparable distinction. Black lily turf, as this perennial is called, slowly produces a dense ground cover of less than 6 inches, combining remarkably well with many flowers and foliages in spring, summer, and winter alike.

CULTURE: Full sun is best for darkest leaf color. Provide ample moisture for optimum establishment.

YEAR-ROUND INTEREST: Summer flowers of lavender on short stems result in glossy, black-purple berries, providing a lovely complement to the foliage.

PLANT COMBINATIONS: An extraordinary number of exciting possibilities exist with this distinctive, unusual plant. Planting it with silver or white variegated foliage yields a dazzling contrast; a more subtle composition is achieved by planting it amid darker foliage and flower colors.

Osmanthus

Osmanthus heterophyllus, a holly look-alike, mixes spiny and smooth-margined leaves on the same plant. It forms a handsome dark green column of foliage to 25 feet or more and supplies a large crop of fragrant white flowers in September and October. **'Variegatus'** is a selection with each leaf neatly rimmed with creamy white. Much slower growing than the standard species, it ultimately produces a shrub to 12 feet. A distinctive cultivar with great potential for winter beauty is **'Purpureus'**, with purplish green winter foliage.

Osmanthus h. **'Goshiki'** has bespeckled foliage of soft yellow and green. The peppering of variegation creates a lovely and bold effect that becomes more pronounced as the shrub slowly gains in size. 'Ogon' has leaves brightly suffused with yellow throughout on plants to 5 feet; it must be sited in partial shade to avoid leaf burn. 'Sasaba' is an outstanding cultivar, with remarkable, spiny, dark green leaves, deeply divided into three separate, overlapping lobes. Look for new cultivars of this species, with distinctive variegation and leaf shape, as they become available in the maritime Northwest.

An infrequently seen species in our area is possibly the most handsome of the genus. *Osmanthus decorus* boasts integrity in foliage and flowers, and the ability to withstand both cold temperatures and summer drought. I have seen neglected specimens in defunct landscapes that looked none the worse for wear. The smooth, linear leaves are medium green and densely cover a compact shrub to 6 feet in height and spread. This species was crossed with O. *delavayi* to produce **O. × burkwoodii** (sometimes still sold as Osmarea × burkwoodii). The hybrid forms an elegant small tree to 15 feet, which, though blossoming freely in early spring, is best grown for its first-rate foliage.

The above-mentioned *Osmanthus delavayi* creates a graceful shrub with 6-foot arching canes covered with small, rounded and toothed leaves of dark green. The natural grace of this species is often ruined by improper pruning and shearing. I have not seen it effectively transformed into a formal clipped hedge, although many gardeners try.

CULTURE: Except for the cultivars noted, *Osmanthus* thrives in full sun as well as in solid shade, where it grows less dense. Once established, it is completely drought-tolerant.

YEAR-ROUND INTEREST: For all too short a period in late April and May, *Osmanthus decorus*, O. × *burkwoodii*, and O. *delavayi* are shrouded in numerous white flowers produced at the base of leaves along the stems. In O. *heterophyllus*, tiny, fragrant white flowers occur in midautumn. The foliage of O. *heterophyllus* 'Purpureus' emerges glossy dark purple in early spring and fades to a purplish green throughout the rest of the year—a useful addition to both winter and summer gardens.

PLANT COMBINATIONS: Integrate these handsome species or any of the cultivars into mixed borders or foundation beds on the north or east side of the house. They tolerate the lack of light that many other plants resent, and still provide fragrance from the spring or autumn flowers. These shrubs also adapt to light woodland conditions, where they compete well with the greedy root systems of native conifers.

Pachistima (Mountain box)

Both species of an evergreen genus known as **Pachistima** can be found occasionally in gardens of the maritime Northwest. The taller (**P. myrsinites**) is a native species that can be found growing alongside, and is often confused with, evergreen huckleberry, *Vaccinium ovatum*. It is not readily available, although specialty nurseries have begun to offer it. Related to *Euonymus* and *Celastrus* (bittersweet), *Pachistima* forms an erect, small shrub cloaked in tiny evergreen leaves similar to those of boxwood. This distinctive and drought-tolerant evergreen is for full to partially shaded conditions in the garden.

Pachistima canbyi, native to eastern North America, best serves the horticulturist, regionalism aside. Densely arranged evergreen leaves cover the branches of this neat and tidy shrublet less than 8 inches tall. It slowly spreads outward, forming a beautiful and textural weed-suppressing ground cover. It is one of few plants that thrive in the nearly intolerable conditions of dry shade created by the Northwest's large conifers.

CULTURE: In full sun to dense shade, these plants are remarkably adaptable to a spectrum of conditions found within our region. Well-drained soils on the dry side are recommended.

YEAR-ROUND INTEREST: In late spring, curiously beautiful maroon flowers are produced in the leaf axils.

PLANT COMBINATIONS: *Pachistima* is ideally suited to creating a ground cover in difficult areas that most plants cannot tolerate. Finely textured foliage creates good contrast with the glossy bold foliage of *Pachysandra Vancouveria* and *Epimedium*.

Pachysandra terminalis

Dense stands of shiny green foliage found in **Pachysandra terminalis**, whorled atop 6-inch stems, create a weedproof perennial ground cover for dry shade. '**Variegata**', a beautiful white-marbled form of this plant, is significantly less vigorous in growth; prepare for several years of coaxing to completely cover any stretch of ground. '**Green Sheen**' has shiny leaves that appear varnished; it carpets as rambunctiously as the standard species.

CULTURE: *Pachysandra* and its cultivars are ideal ground covers for fully shaded sites, though with ample moisture they will tolerate bright, partially shaded situations. Plant on 8-inch centers for a dense carpet in two growing seasons.

YEAR-ROUND INTEREST: Terminal stubby spikes of creamy white are produced in early spring.

PLANT COMBINATIONS: The dense evergreen carpet this species provides will carry a bed through the winter, even if the focal plants are deciduous.

Quercus (Oak)

Although there are a large number of useful candidates, broad-leaved evergreen trees are sadly and inexplicably ignored in our landscapes. Evergreen oaks, *Quercus*, and their relatives (including *Castanopsis chrysophylla*, below) have served a small and select following throughout the Pacific Northwest, and for good reason.

Quercus ilex, the Holm oak, is sturdy and tough, with slightly toothed hollylike leaves on a round-crowned tree to 45 feet. Similar in size but gray-green in foliage is **Q. suber**, commonly called the cork oak. Throughout the Mediterranean region, which in its summer dryness is similar in climate to that of the maritime Northwest, groves of its thick, spongy, gray-brown trunks are harvested for the cork of commerce. The marvelous textural qualities of this bark also can be "harvested"—tactilely and visually—for enjoyment in the landscape. Its year-round foliage and tidy growth habit are other bonuses.

Quercus glauca and **Q. myrsinifolia** each become small, yet handsome and distinctive, evergreen trees or large shrubs to 20 feet. Their glossy green leaves also remain comely throughout the year. The leaves of *Q. glauca* are nearly oval, with smooth margins, whereas *Q. myrsinifolia* has more linear leaves with somewhat jagged edges. **Quercus hypoleucoides**, to 35 feet, has linear leaves that are dark green above, with an intensely white undercoating of fine, woolly hair. This effect is quite marvelous when observed from under the tree.

Distinctive and deserving of greater recognition is a Northwestern native oak relative known as the golden chinquapin, **Castanopsis chrysophylla**. It produces a tidy, intensely dark green, mounded specimen of 30 feet in height with a striking leaf undercoating of rich gold. The seed of *Castanopsis*, like that of the chestnuts, comes enclosed in a spiny burr instead of the acorn typical of this family.

CULTURE: True oaks and their relatives thrive in well-drained positions of full sun, with no supplemental summer water. These species are ideal to include in the garden for their drought tolerance. Oaks and their relatives resent transplanting after establishment, so give them a permanent site when young. Avoid trying to grow them in higher elevations with consistent low winter temperatures.

YEAR-ROUND INTEREST: Foliage is superb throughout the calendar. New growth of the evergreen oaks is red, providing a colorful spring seasonal effect.

PLANT COMBINATIONS: Consider using as an anchor for a bed of rockroses or as an exemplary lawn specimen. The smaller evergreen oak species are ideal as foundation plantings or integrated into the mixed shrubbery border with flowering shrubs and small trees.

Viburnum (Viburnum)

The evergreen viburnums are perhaps the most useful shrubs available to year-round gardeners of the maritime Northwest. Collectively, this genus provides twelve months of interest from foliage, flowers, and fruit. By carefully selecting and integrating several species into your garden, you can profit from the strengths of each. The richness of foliage alone that this large genus provides is nearly unmatched elsewhere in the plant kingdom.

Viburnum awabuki var. *chindo* has upright rusty-colored stems to 6 feet, to which are attached bold, glossy green 8-inch leaves. During the winter, this hardy species provides remarkable contrast of foliage. In midsummer, fragrant rounded trusses of flowers blossom abundantly on older plants, followed by red fruits.

The commonly planted **Viburnum davidii** matures no taller than 3 feet high and 5 feet wide. Late-autumn through early-spring blossoms, nestled among the foliage, often result in robin's-egg-blue fruit. A well-grown stand competes in ornament with any rarity we may put it up against, although overuse has given it an undeserved reputation for vulgarity. If you take V. *davidii* and wish it tall, dark, and more handsome, you will have **V. cinnamomifolium**. It is a striking addition to the larger garden, worthy of planting for its foliage that is nearly identical to that of V. *davidii* but on stems reaching nearly 8 feet in height.

One of the most beautiful viburnums in foliage is **Viburnum × pragense**, whose dark green polish makes it sparkle in the winter sun. The foliage of this 6-foot-tall hardy hybrid shrub is reason enough to include it in the garden. Ivorine flowers are produced in late spring. One of its parents, **V. rhytidophyllum**, is by itself a handsome foliage plant if grown under the right conditions. The narrow, leathery, and deeply veined leaves provide a wonderful textural component for Northwest winter landscapes but if given too much sun will often scorch and become unsightly.

CULTURE: The evergreen viburnums are best sited in moist and rich soil, in full sun to partial shade. (Note individual species' requirements in the above text.)

YEAR-ROUND INTEREST: Flowers and fruit are produced, as noted with each individual species.

PLANT COMBINATIONS: There are no finer foliage plants in the garden. Use as a background to offset winter-flowering plants, or integrate into the mixed border or foundation plantings around the house.

Blossoms of Winter: Flowers

The offering of flowers in the depth of winter is what we most cherish from our dormant gardens, perhaps because it seems so unexpected. Yet many plant species find much less competition for attention from visiting pollinators during this time than during the fray of high summer, when the market value of nectar takes a nose dive. Whatever its biological cause, this off-season approach to the process of procreation provides the gardener moments of marveling at the sight and fragrance of the winter flower.

The familiar perfume of witch hazels and sarcococca combines with the bite of the winter air to offer a refreshing and awakening promise that the assault has been met and resisted. These plants, along with the common winter bulbs, such as galanthus, winter aconite, and crocus, are the standard bearers of winter. Yet there are multitudes more of both woody and herbaceous plants that exploit the quietness of winter by presenting their floral display.

TREES AND SHRUBS

Abeliophyllum distichum (White forsythia)

Known commonly as white forsythia, **Abeliophyllum distichum** is not truly a forsythia, but it is a distant relation. I appreciate this shrub for both the nearly black 4-foot stems and the small, white, four-petaled flowers that open in February. Hailing from the much warmer summer climate of Korea, white forsythia seemingly languishes in the cool maritime Northwest climate. However, both the species and its pink cultivar, **A. distichum** 'Roseum', present a few stems of early color during the last days of dreary winter. You can force them into blossom quite easily by bringing the cut stems indoors.

37

CULTURE: Plant in a warm location in full sun or partial shade, and provide supplemental summer water for optimum growth.

YEAR-ROUND INTEREST: The black stems of this species are attractive when out of blossom, though it becomes a rather nondescript shrub after the foliage appears.

PLANT COMBINATIONS: Site in front of a dark background for optimum viewing when in blossom. Consider allowing the stems to emerge from a ground cover of deep green, such as *Waldsteinia ternata*, or the black foliage of the grasslike *Ophiopogon planiscapus* 'Nigrescens'.

Azara microphylla (Box-leaf azara)

The box-leaf azara, **Azara microphylla**, is a finely textured evergreen shrub or small tree (to 20 feet) that has thrived in the Pacific Northwest for many years. In very early spring, small greenish yellow flowers blossom on this species and its less-encountered cultivar, **A. microphylla 'Variegata'**. Because of its wispy texture, plant *Azara* in groups of three or five to enhance the overall impact. Place it where you can enjoy the remarkable fragrance of white chocolate during late winter.

CULTURE: This species tends to become a bit lanky as it matures, so selectively prune to encourage a more comely appearance. Summer irrigation encourages more robust growth although it is drought-tolerant once established. Harsh winters cause stem dieback and loss of flower buds, so site where it is protected from drying winds.

YEAR-ROUND INTEREST: Throughout the year, the small and rounded leaves of the species remain glossed, finely textured, and dark green. The tiny leaves of its extremely rare but choice cultivar 'Variegata' are boldly bordered in creamy white.

PLANT COMBINATIONS: Integrate this evergreen into the mixed border or use as a foundation planting.

Berberis (Barberry)

Two species of **Berberis** (barberries) demonstrate their talents beyond berry and foliage through the character of their winter flowers.

It is always delightful to come across the bright orange blossoms of **Berberis darwinii**, which Charles Darwin first discovered during his momentous voyage around the tip of South America. **B. darwinii** is a true winter-blossoming species, and one of the few species to produce rich orange flowers rather than the typical yellow usually found in the barberries. The small and spiny foliage of dark green contrasts richly with the flowers formed from late autumn into midwinter. This arching shrub grows to 7 feet in height and width.

Berberis linearifolia is a choice species that deserves more attention for use in our climate as a distinctive and beautiful winter-blossoming shrub, to 6 feet in height. In late winter, the arching canes of this elegant evergreen are covered with brilliant orange flowers that are nearly fluorescent if hit by a direct stroke of winter sun.

CULTURE: Evergreen barberries tolerate shade but require bright conditions for best growth and flowering. Remove awkward branches at ground level rather than making heading cuts. New branches arise from the base to replace those you remove.

YEAR-ROUND INTEREST: You will appreciate the rich foliage of these species throughout the calendar. Blue berries are produced in midsummer, although the deciduous barberry species are more reliable for this effect in the maritime Northwest (see Chapter 6, "Berries").

PLANT COMBINATIONS: Because the bright orange flowers appear at a time when little else is happening in the garden, the possibility of clashing colors is diminished. This shrub is often still in flower when the red-orange foliage of *Spiraea* x *bumalda* 'Goldflame' emerges, creating a scene of remarkable harmony. Use barberries in your winter perennial border or integrate them into the foundation beds surrounding your house.

Camellia (Camellia)

In the Northwest, we are blessed with the opportunity to grow a large number of species and hybrids of **Camellia**, whose natural homelands of Japan, Korea, China, and the lower Himalaya have climates similar to ours. There are over 20,000 named cultivars, from several species and hybrids, from which you can select many that respond admirably to our maritime Northwest climate.

In late autumn, **Camellia sinensis** scatters among its dark green foliage lovely and simple single white flowers with an elusive fragrance. Considering the hardiness of this species and its apparent contentedness with our climate, it surprises me how rarely this 6-foot shrub is encountered in Northwest landscapes. The dependable flowers bloom from mid-October through December. The leaves of this species are plucked when young and dried to produce tea.

The hardiest camellia, **Camellia oleifera**, is the commercial source of tea oil. In early November, this Chinese camellia produces lovely single white flowers, generally larger than those of C. *sinensis*, on a shrub that grows to 5 feet tall. This species is among the most dependable of the flowering camellias during the colder Northwest winters.

Camellia sasanqua, from the southern islands of Japan, is an elegant species that is put to good use in the maritime Northwest. Slightly more tender than the more common C. *japonica*, it needs a somewhat protected area, in shade or semishade. The biggest advantage by far of this species is its propensity to drop its individual flower petals— unlike the ubiquitous C. *japonica*, whose flowers remain attached long after they have lost their beauty. Although *sasanqua* cultivars run into the thousands, the vast majority of those available are the elegant, single-flowered forms in soft shades of white and pink. Select your specimens when they are in blossom by visiting nurseries in mid-November and December.

A scarce hybrid known as **Camellia × williamsii** has long been grown in the Northwest and is among the most acceptable of the larger-flowering camellias. This English hybrid has an open habit and flowers that, like those of its parent C. *sasanqua*, shatter and drop after flowering. The best of the C. *saluensis* blood of the other parent is in the relatively large flower size and glossy leaves. Of the several selections made from this hybrid cross, **C. × williamsii 'Donation'** is perhaps the best known in the maritime Northwest, with incredible numbers of rich, pink semidouble flowers produced during late winter.

CULTURE: Camellias are by nature woodland plants; however, on the islands of Japan *Camellia japonica* is often found growing in open scrub near the ocean, and in our climate it tolerates full sun better than other species. Give your camellias the benefit of a rich, organic, moist soil and a yearly application of rhododendron fertilizer.

YEAR-ROUND INTEREST: In autumn, observe the curious green fruit containing large black seeds. By carefully selecting several species and hybrids, you can have flowers from late September through May.

PLANT COMBINATIONS: Consider planting camellias among a semi-shaded mixed border of evergreen and deciduous shrubs, or along the north or east foundation of your house. The mid- to late-winter-blossoming selections in soft pink enliven the garden if planted with the soft pastel yellows of *Stachyurus praecox* or the unrestrained glaring yellow of most *Forsythia*. The dark green and glossy foliage is also a perfect foil for many late-spring and early-summer-blossoming shrubs, such as *Philadelphus*, *Deutzia*, *Weigela*, *Itea*, and *Hydrangea*.

Chimonanthus praecox (Wintersweet)

On a brisk late-January day, I am often overwhelmed with garden air awash in the fragrance of **Chimonanthus praecox**, commonly referred to as wintersweet. Its winter charm awakens when it brandishes an abundance of drooping, waxy yellow flowers with a sweet, fruity scent. **C. praecox var. luteus** has flowers of rich yellow that are effective from some distance, unlike the rather dull yellowish white of the standard form.

CULTURE: Find a sunny or semishaded position in the garden where this plant will be appreciated during the winter months.

YEAR-ROUND INTEREST: Use as a support for summer-blossoming vines, such as *Clematis* or *Tropaeolum speciosum*.

PLANT COMBINATIONS: Place in a mixed border, with winter- and summer-blossoming shrubs as well as herbaceous perennials and bulbs, near an entrance to your home. Such a siting lets you appreciate the plant's fragrance yet allows its ungainly appearance to fade during the summer months.

Corylopsis (Winter hazel)

From early winter until after the vernal equinox, numerous species of **Corylopsis**, the winter hazels, offer a continual source of fragrant, pastel yellow flowers on shrubs well suited to partially shaded landscapes. The earliest to flower and the most frequently encountered in our landscapes, **Corylopsis pauciflora**, is the smallest of the species, producing a low-spreading plant of 5 feet in height and breadth. The species name *pauciflora* refers to the few flowers (1–3) of each inflorescence rather than to the paucity of flowers on the shrub as a whole. The lemon yellow blossoms are sweetly scented, yet far from overpowering. Provide a position sheltered from the sun to avoid unsightly scorched leaves.

As the flowers of *Corylopsis pauciflora* start to fade in mid-March, those of **C. spicata** are just appearing. This is a large species, to 10 feet, with bold or toothed foliage and crowded clusters of soft yellow flowers that partially expose a tuft of red stamens. Later in March, **C. sinensis**, the Chinese winter hazel, produces large, drooping clusters of up to 15 yellow flowers with orange-red stamens, on even taller upright stems.

From late March to early April, naked stems of **Corylopsis glabrescens** bear flowers on drooping spikes to 2 inches in length. The foliage emerges with a wonderful bronze green and later takes on a hint of blue. C. *glabrescens* stays below 8 feet in height.

CULTURE: The winter hazels are a good choice for a lightly shaded position, although C. *glabrescens* tolerates full sun. Irrigate in summer until fully established to avoid leaf scald, which may occur if the shrub is given too hot a situation. As with so many flowering shrubs, when pruning the larger species, remove the entire branch to the ground rather than heading back (which results in awkward growth and destroys the natural grace of the shrub).

YEAR-ROUND INTEREST: The soft yellow autumn color is generally nothing to write home about.

PLANT COMBINATIONS: Soft pastel yellow flowers of the winter hazels make them ideal companions to many early-blossoming species. Soft pink or purple hellebores are a perfect complement. The blues of early-blossoming *Pulmonaria*, *Chionodoxa*, and *Lathyrus vernus* also provide a pleasing visual union. Adding the bright purple flowers of *Rhododendron mucronulatum* to the scene can be quite striking.

Daphne (Daphne)

Among the most beautiful and fragrant of shrubs are the many species of **Daphne**, which can, by themselves, provide year-round effect in foliage and flowers. At the base of the steps which lead off my deck is planted **D. blagayana**, consistently the first of this genus to blossom in the Pacific Northwest. The flowers often open fully during sharp late-February frosts, in the still air of a warm late-winter afternoon, saturating the garden with fragrance. Use it most effectively by pairing it with another ground cover because the plant soon produces a barren center.

Daphne laureola, the spurge laurel, grows 2 or 3 feet high, producing greenish yellow flowers in axillary clusters along its stems, in late February through March. Although these flowers are often hidden by the striking, waxy green foliage, they are fragrant during the evening. I am partial to the dwarf **D. laureola var. philippi**, which forms dense tufts of glossy foliage to 6 inches and intermittently fragrant flowers during late winter. Few plants are more shade-tolerant.

Daphne odora, the winter daphne, is a mounded evergreen shrub. In midwinter it produces exceptionally fragrant flowers of white or pink, depending upon the cultivar, in clusters borne on the branch tips.

With a personality that is somewhat less demanding, but an equally good choice for late-winter flowers, is **Daphne mezereum**, a very hardy deciduous species, known as the February daphne. For several weeks in February and March, the upright, barren 4-foot stems are covered with fragrant, rich purple flowers. The cultivar **D. *mezerum*** **'Alba'** produces white flowers.

CULTURE: The ultimate performance of the daphnes seems to depend upon several factors in combination, making its success an exercise based partly in luck and partly in knowledge. Except for *D. mezereum* and *D. blagayana*, members of the genus described above resent full sun and require a rich loamy soil with little summer irrigation. Regardless of the conditions and care provided, daphnes often expire suddenly without apparent reason. However, their matchless winter fragrance makes them worth a gamble.

YEAR-ROUND INTEREST: Although they are quite striking, the red or black ripe fruits that follow the blossom period are poisonous. Fortunately, *Daphne mezereum* and *D. laureola* are the only prolific fruiters of those daphnes mentioned. The dark green, unblemished leaves of *D. laureola* also make a very handsome foliage plant throughout the year. The cultivar *D. odora* 'Aureomarginata' sports leaves with a yellow margin, providing a season of interest after blossoming.

PLANT COMBINATIONS: When *Daphne blagayana*, with its terminal clusters of creamy, fragrant flowers, is planted among the red fruit of *Gaultheria procumbens*, the effect is a treasure of diamonds and rubies at the end of February. *D. mezereum* produces its rich lavender blossoms when the earliest daffodils are in blossom and combines quite potently with their rich golds and yellows.

Erica (Heath)

For an effective showing of winter color, as well as for the sheer number of flowers produced, few shrubs compare with the species and hybrids of the genus **Erica**, the heaths. Although the true heathers, genus *Calluna*, extend the season of this group of plants into late summer and early autumn, only true heaths provide color from late autumn through the height of summer. Hundreds of selections are available, in mind-boggling diversity. A few standard cultivars are mentioned below: explore in your nursery the incredible spectrum of colors and textures provided by these plants.

In late autumn and early winter, the Mediterranean heaths, **Erica × darleyensis**, provide multitudes of small bell-like flowers on white (**E. × darleyensis 'Silberschmelze'**) or pink (**E. × darleyensis 'Darley Dale'**). Both ultimately produce a 2-foot rounded mound of tiny, dark green needlelike leaves and stems crowded with light green flower buds.

Lower growing are the late winter-blossoming cultivars of **Erica carnea**, which offer greater choices of color. In overlapping sequence with the Mediterranean heaths, **E. carnea 'King George'** is spangled with deep magenta flowers among dark purplish foliage in early January. Two standard cultivars, **'Springwood'** (white flowers) and **'Springwood Pink'**, display their blossoms from early March through June. This species ultimately produces mats of low-growing stems spreading 3 feet wide but generally not growing taller than 1 foot.

Two larger species, known as the tree heaths, are remarkable late-winter-blossoming shrubs, eventually reaching 8 to 10 feet. **Erica lusitanica** blossoms in late February with fragrant, pinkish-white flowers, and **E. arborea var. arborea** fills March with white flowers.

CULTURE: Heaths grow best in full sun in acidic, well-prepared soils, and need adequate moisture during summer. They resent heavy soils that drain poorly; no standing water should be present after rain or irrigation. Sharply shear stems after flowering each year to stimulate new growth from the base. Left unpruned, these shrubs ultimately produce barren centers that will not regenerate from the base.

YEAR-ROUND INTEREST: By careful selection, you can have the heaths (Erica) and heathers (Calluna) in blossom twelve months of the year. Both genera require the same growing conditions. The needlelike foliage of the heaths is attractive year-round, and forms a dense weed-smothering ground cover in full sun if frequently pruned.

PLANT COMBINATIONS: The heaths and heathers are excellent with dwarf conifers, providing color during the winter months, and contrast to the foliage and flowers of their blossoming companions during the summer months. For greater visual impact, plant several of each cultivar in groups.

Garrya (Coast silk tassel)

A wonderful addition to any Northwest garden is **Garrya elliptica**, a large evergreen shrub native to western North America, which deserves much wider recognition by horticulturists and garden designers alike. In early winter, when our landscapes are still plagued by bitter cold and snow, curtains of dangling greenish white catkins are produced from branches cloaked with leathery evergreen foliage. Select **G. elliptica 'James Roof'** for its showy, extremely long male catkins, up to 12 inches. When a male plant is present, female plants yield waxy purple fruit that ripens in late summer.

Garrya × *issaquahensis*, which first occurred in a private garden in Issaquah, Washington, is a hybrid between G. *elliptica* and a hardier inland species from Oregon and California. In my estimation, it makes a landscape plant superior to G. *elliptica* and its selected cultivars. It, too, has elegant drooping catkins of significant length in early winter, yet the hardiness of its G. *fremontii* parent expands the areas in which this shrub can be grown. In years when temperatures dip into the single digits, this hybrid performs unscathed, whereas the foliage and flowers of G. *elliptica* are often damaged.

CULTURE: Site all garryas in full sun to partial shade, in well-drained soils. Summer water is unnecessary after they are established. They are salt- and wind-tolerant.

YEAR-ROUND INTEREST: If both sexes are present, look for waxy purple fruit in drooping clusters on female plants during the summer months. Handsome gray-green foliage on maroon-colored stems is held throughout the year.

PLANT COMBINATIONS: Horizontal lines of prostrate junipers planted at the base of garrya can heighten the effect of the vertically drooping catkins produced in midwinter. Add garrya to the sunny perennial border for strength and interest during the off season.

Hamamelis (Witch hazel)

The royalty of winter-blossoming plants are in the genus **Hamamelis**, the witch hazels. Few hardy shrubs offer such elegance in winter flower, entrancing fragrance, and enduring toughness. Although there are native American species available, the Asiatic members of this genus are among the most appealing.

Hamamelis japonica forms a large multistemmed shrub, and its winter branches produce wrinkled, spidery flowers of golden yellow, starting as early as mid-January. The Chinese counterpart, **H. mollis**, is the monarch of the lot and the most deserving of inclusion in our gardens. Large, golden yellow flowers, composed of numerous narrow petals, release an enchanting and pervasive sweetness throughout the winter landscape. The cultivar **H. mollis** 'Primavera' features broader petals of light yellow and is superior to the older mainstay, **H. mollis** 'Pallida'.

The blue-blooded offspring of these two Asiatic parents have expanded unbelievably the breadth of beauty achievable from the witch hazels. Of the many fine golden-flowered selections from this cross,

Hamamelis × *intermedia* 'Arnold's Promise' remains a favorite, with very twiggy, upright growth and densely packed flowers of rich yellow opening in late February and early March. The bright yellow flowers in heavy clusters of **H.** × *intermedia* 'Sunburst' are considered superior for both the dependability of blossom and the bonus of heady fragrance.

Fine dark red flowers are presented by *Hamamelis* × *intermedia* 'Diane' and **H.** × *intermedia* 'Ruby Glow'. Yet their finest seasonal ornament is not the dark flowers, in my estimation, but the incredible blendings of orange and red that make up their autumn foliage. The flowers possess a subtle beauty, but they are too dark to be effective at a distance; so site them, if possible, where they can be backlit.

The lovely orange cultivars, including *Hamamelis* × *intermedia* 'Winter Beauty' and **H.** × *intermedia* 'Jelena', are exceptional for floral beauty, as well as fragrance. 'Winter Beauty' blossoms as early as mid-December, adding a waft of delicious scent to the air as I scurry about cleaning the perennial beds from summer's end. Depending upon the weather, 'Jelena' blossoms from the first of the year onwards to February, with somewhat larger flowers of rich orange.

CULTURE: Witch hazels thrive in either full sun or partial shade. Provide a rich organic soil, although they tolerate a wide range of soil types.

YEAR-ROUND INTEREST: Autumn color! The yellow-, orange-, and red-flowering cultivars tend to echo the same respective shades in their autumn leaf display.

PLANT COMBINATIONS: The beauty of the brighter-flowering types can be appreciated from a great distance if they are placed in front of a dark background, such as the dark, pendulous foliage of the Northwest's native hemlock, *Tsuga heterophylla*. Site the darker orange and red cultivars where you can appreciate their flowering season from a closer range. The darker-flowering cultivars are also quite effective when combined with the brighter species and cultivars.

Helleborus (Hellebore)

Four widely available *Helleborus* species will briefly introduce you to the marvelous potential found within this incredible genus. Few winter-flowering plants stir my blood with more fervor than this distinctive and distinguished group of plants.

Helleborus argutifolius has spiny, gray-green trifoliate leaves on upright stems to 4 feet in height. In very early winter, a crown of lime green flowers is produced atop the stems. Because the petals remain attached long after pollination has occurred, the season of effectiveness is extended for many weeks throughout the winter and early spring.

More finely textured in foliage than *Helleborus argutifolius* is the stinking hellebore, **H. foetidus**, named for the scent of its leaves when bruised. It produces 2-foot stems of dark blue-green dissected foliage. Seemingly no matter how brutish the winter, dense, light green flowering shoots unfurl in January to produce large clusters of tightly closed green flowers rimmed in red. Some specimens offer a distinctive and sweet fragrance from the opened flowers.

Helleborus niger, the Christmas rose, is oddly quite scarce in our climate for no reason other than its lower likelihood to produce quantities of seeds. The Christmas rose produces a clump of foliage and flowers that rises directly from a crown below soil surface. Elegant white flowers are borne singly on each stem, which begins to thrust upwards in late January (despite its common name). The beauty of blossom increases each year as the clump gains in breadth.

Of the more commonly available species, the most interest is currently directed towards the Lenten rose, known as **Helleborus × orientalis**. As with *H. niger*, the flowering stems emerge from the ground, but with several flowers on each stem. The Lenten rose offers the most variation in color, from near black and blue-black through reds, pinks, primrose yellow, and bespeckled whites. More flowering stems are produced each year, eventually becoming crowded clumps of color that remain effective from late January through most of April. The petals never actually fall, but simply fade over time, so the effect from these flowers can extend into June.

CULTURE: Both *Helleborus niger* and *H. × orientalis* are heavy feeders that respond to a well-worked soil, with organic matter added at the time of planting. *H. niger* enjoys more alkaline conditions than other species but thrives in our slightly acidic native soils. The stemmed hellebores seem more forgiving in regard to soil and are less likely to topple from the weight of winter snow if underfed and underwatered during the growing season. The stems of *H. argutifolius* and *H. foetidus* flower only once, and should be removed after new growth appears from the base, unless you wish to collect seeds for additional plants. Cut off old foliage early in the season, as it generally appears bedraggled after a year's wear.

YEAR-ROUND INTEREST: The foliage of the hellebores adds substance to the garden long after blossoming.

PLANT COMBINATIONS: The possibilities are endless, with myriad colors of each species complementing other hellebores and additional winter-blossoming plants. The bright green-yellow flowers of the stemmed species work wonderfully with the lavender-pink to bright purple flowers of *Rhododendron mucronulatum*, which blossoms concurrently. I prefer putting the dark pinks and red-blacks of the *orientalis* hybrids with the soft pastel yellows of *Corylopsis*, *Stachyurus*, and *Primula veris* (cowslips). The pure whites work with darker reds, as well as with the blackish foliage of *Ophiopogon planiscapus* 'Nigrescens'.

Jasminum nudiflorum (Winter-blooming jasmine)

Surprisingly rare in Northwest cultivation is the winter-blossoming jasmine, *Jasminum nudiflorum*. Unfortunately lacking the pervasive scent of many other jasmine species, in mid- to late winter this deciduous shrub presents a colorful display of tubular, bright yellow flowers borne on arching green stems. The growth habit lends itself to covering sunny slopes or espaliering against a southern wall, where it is in blossom as early as mid-January.

CULTURE: Although this forgiving plant tolerates dryness during the summer, it needs supplemental summer watering until well established.

YEAR-ROUND INTEREST: The arching green canes are attractive all year, as are the fresh green leaves during the summer months.

PLANT COMBINATIONS: Plant this jasmine species on a trellis in combination with a deciduous summer-blossoming vine such as *Clematis*. This provides two seasons of colorful flowers in the same space.

Lindera obtusiloba

Lindera obtusiloba, a multistemmed deciduous tree related to sassafras and California bay, covers its branches in early spring with small clusters of golden flowers that from a distance somewhat resemble *Cornus mas*. The boldly lobed leaves, 5 to 7 inches in length, emerge in spring with a reddish tone turning to rich green throughout summer. This tall shrub, ultimately growing to 25 feet in height, is profoundly underused in our urban gardens.

CULTURE: Grow in partial shade. Cool moist soil is best, although this species tolerates moderate soil dryness.

YEAR-ROUND INTEREST: Fresh and bold green summer foliage changes to intense, clear yellow in autumn. Crops of shiny black fruit are produced on female plants in October and November when both sexes are present.

Top: Hoarfrost coats evergreen *Cotoneaster* foliage. **Middle:** *Leucothoe fontanesiana* 'Rainbow' combines effectively with dwarf giant sequoia and many species of evergreen *Gaultheria*. **Bottom left:** Leaves of *Nandina domestica* 'Nana'—a dwarf heavenly bamboo—take on red and yellow in winter. **Bottom right, top:** Ubiquitous *Bergenia cordifolia* lends beauty in rich purple. **Bottom right, bottom:** *Ophiopogon planiscapus* 'Nigrescens' echoes the rock color (Bloedel Reserve).

Top, left and right: Spicy fragrance comes with colorful witch hazels, December through March. Consider yellow *Hamamelis mollis* and rich red-orange *H. x intermedia* 'Diane'. **Bottom:** Heaths provide floral color from October through August. *Erica carnea* 'Springwood White' and 'King George' bloom in winter.

Top: *Chimonanthus praecox* lends its fruity, heavy scent to the winter garden in late January. **Middle:** *Jasminum nudiflorum* offers a different shade of yellow from late January through March. **Bottom:** *Galanthus* is one of many standard winter-blooming bulbs that complement winter plantings from January through April.

Top right: Flowers of *Stachyurus praecox* grace burgundy branchlets in February. **Top left:** In the same month, *Camellia* x *williamsii* brings to gardens the boldness of common *C. japonica*, but with petals that drop when spent. **Bottom:** Striking red trusses of *Rhododendron strigillosum* also appear in February.

Late winter delivers the first flash of color from woodland herbs. **Top:** The flowers of *Helleborus* x *orientalis* are effective from late February to late April. **Bottom:** During the same period, *Pulmonaria angustifolia* presents rich blue flowers.

Both deciduous and evergreen shrubs lend berry color to winter. **Top:** *Skimmia japonica* amid glossy foliage. **Middle:** *Iris foetidissima* is grown not for flowers but for striking fruit that persists from late autumn to early winter. **Bottom:** *Ilex verticillata* is an effective deciduous holly.

Top: *Pernettya mucronata* displays pink berries in early January. **Middle:** *Cotoneaster horizontalis* adds color to a fence all winter. **Bottom:** *Stranvaesia davidiana* on a frosty day.

Top left: A stripebark maple, *Acer tegmentosum*. **Middle left:** *A. griseum*. **Bottom left:** *Cornus kousa*. **Top right:** *Salix purpurea* 'Nana', left, with C. *alba* 'Kelseyi' in front; the red bark of C. *alba* 'Elegantissima', center; *Kerria japonica*, right (author's garden). **Bottom right:** A maple bark covered in moss, *Erica carnea* flowers amid evergreen foliage, and berries of *Cotoneaster* (Kubota Gardens).

PLANT COMBINATIONS: Site in a moderately shaded position with a dark background of conifers to enhance the early spring blossoms of rich yellow. Planting with *Styrax*, *Stewartia*, and *Cornus* (dogwoods) establishes a progression of blossoms that carries a corner of the garden from early March through late June.

Lonicera (Honeysuckle)

Deliciously scented and colorful tubular flowers are found on both shrubs and vines of the genus *Lonicera*—the honeysuckles. Two shrubby species, as well as the hybrid between them, are notable for the quantity of flowers produced from December through March which, although not showy, are powerfully fragrant.

Lonicera fragrantissima forms an arching and somewhat suckering shrub to 8 feet in height, and remains partially evergreen during the winter months. From late December through March, a steady supply of small, white flowers are produced along the stems to atomize the winter air with spicy, sweet perfume. If hard winter frosts damage the flowers, they are quickly replaced by densely packed flower buds waiting in line to blossom.

Lonicera standishii has somewhat smaller flowers and bristly stems when young, but otherwise differs only slightly from *L. fragrantissima*. The hybrid between the two, **L. × purpusii**, is somewhat more floriferous than the parents, producing quantities of exceedingly fragrant flowers for four months in the depth of winter. Like its parents, it reaches nearly 8 feet in height and forms a rather upright arching shrub.

CULTURE: All three honeysuckles perform equally in full sun or partial shade, and respond well to pruning. They are reasonably drought-tolerant once established.

YEAR-ROUND INTEREST: Little to none.

PLANT COMBINATIONS: Position honeysuckle upwind from the areas of the garden you use most during the winter months. Incorporate into the mixed shrubbery, along with summer-blossoming shrubs and conifers. Allow a clematis to scramble from the base of the honeysuckle through its limbs, providing a false season of color to the otherwise summer-dull foliage.

Mahonia

Mahonia species differ from the closely related *Berberis* by having compound, rather than simple, leaves. The aristocratic Asiatic species and hybrids are among the most effective winter-blossoming shrubs to include in any garden.

Mahonia × *media* 'Charity' produces bold, luxuriant foliage and soft yellow flowers on erect spikes in late February. Other cultivars of the same parents (M. *japonica* and M. *lomariifolia*) include 'Lionel Fortescue', 'Hope', 'Cantab', and 'Underway', all of which produce lovely upright and fragrant yellow racemes in the depths of winter.

Mahonia × *'Arthur Menzies'* is an early-blossoming cross between *Mahonia bealei*, a late bloomer with the least effective flower, and M. *lomariifolia*. 'Arthur Menzies' originated in a flat of seedlings from Strybing Arboretum in San Francisco, and was selected at Washington Park Arboretum in Seattle. It produces lovely 15-inch upright racemes of bright yellow flowers, often in blossom by New Year's Day. Well known among Seattle plant enthusiasts, this striking small tree deserves much greater attention by gardeners of the maritime Northwest.

CULTURE: Mahonias require shelter from both hot sun and extremely cold temperatures; beneath a high canopy of native conifers is ideal. They benefit from summer irrigation but tolerate dry summers once fully established. Severely prune all young specimens after flowering to increase the number of stems produced from the base.

YEAR-ROUND INTEREST: Enormous bacchian clusters of dusted blue berries hang from mahonias in midsummer, following the early March blossom season. The spiny bold green foliage is evergreen, though in full sun will develop beautiful red autumn color.

PLANT COMBINATIONS: Few sights are more beautiful to come across in the dead of winter than a mature specimen of any winter-flowering *Mahonia* in blossom. Use singly, or group for more impact from the pastel yellow flowers in vertical trusses. Mahonia works well when planted with the soft pink flowers of *Camellia* 'Donation'. A rich black-green carpet of *Sarcococca ruscifolia* at the base creates a bold contrast to the mahonia's spiny medium green leaves.

Prunus (Cherry and Apricot)

The winter-flowering cherry, *Prunus subhirtella* 'Autumnalis Rosea', is almost an emblem of our benign maritime climate, and is a beloved member of the winter-flowering family. It usually begins blossoming during late autumn, and continues unchecked throughout the winter in all but our coldest weather. Delicate, soft pink flowers continually emerge from a host of buds that lie in wait for their turn to open. The darker-flowered **P. subhirtella** 'Whitcombii' (= 'Rosea') has richer pink blossoms and often waits until late February or early March to begin flowering.

Over the centuries, Japanese poets and artists have immortalized the flowering stems of **Prunus mume**, which speak of the soft and gentle awakening of spring. The Japanese flowering apricot is a lovely February-blossoming tree with large and deliciously fragrant single or double flowers of rich reds, pinks, or pure white (depending upon the cultivar).

CULTURE: With this obligatory and benevolent introduction completed, I must now dish the dirt on these trees by discussing their character in seasons of foliage. Brown rot, a common fungus that causes severe twig dieback, enters the plant through the flowers during periods of wetness. Despite their beauty during the winter months, I admit there are longer-lived and more suitable trees for the Northwest garden.

YEAR-ROUND INTEREST: Firewood.

PLANT COMBINATIONS: Underplant with *Rhododendron mucronulatum* or *R.* 'Praecox' ; they blossom concurrently, with complementing purple hues. Early-blossoming crocus and primula also provide a ground-covering echo of the color of these trees in early spring.

Rhododendron (Rhododendron)

Visit nurseries and public gardens throughout the winter and early spring to introduce yourself to the early-blossoming species and hybrids of the genus **Rhododendron**.

The first winter bloomer is the deciduous **Rhododendron mucronulatum**. This medium-sized, spreading shrub, to 6 feet in height, produces quantities of soft lavender blossoms from December to March. It lightens the dourness of this season by offering wave after wave of flowers, even after hard freezes. A pure white-flowering form, **'Album'**, is available, as is a large-flowered and richly colored selection called **'Cornell Pink'**. Seedling-grown plants of this species are variable —purchase them while in flower. This species performs equally well in partial shade or in full sun, where its foliage will turn rich tones of orange, red, and yellow before falling.

Semievergreen in the maritime Northwest is **Rhododendron dauricum**, a species valued for its lavender to reddish purple flowers produced during warm spells throughout the winter, starting in late February. Its most notable offspring, **R. 'Praecox'**, is a remarkably hardy shrub to 5 feet in height, which produces multitudes of rich purple-pink flowers in early March and plum-colored foliage throughout the calendar. The other 'Praecox' parent, **R. ciliatum**, is worthy of cultivating for early blossom. It creates a mounded, tidy evergreen shrub with medium-sized leaves coated underneath with small, closely set hairs. The rose-pink flowers open from reddish pink buds in late March.

The middle of March sees blossoms of **Rhododendron moupinense**, a delightful species with large tubular flowers of pinkish white opening from buds of deeper shading. It creates a low spreading shrub to 3 feet. *Rhododendron moupinense* was crossed with R. *dauricum*, resulting in **R. 'Olive'**, which is valued for large, rich pink flowers in late February and early March.

Rhododendron strigillosum is one of my favorites for early March, not only for the intensely colored trusses of deep red flowers but for the elegant narrow foliage held in dense whorls from distinctively hairy stems. It produces a shrub to 6 feet in height that is striking in full blossom.

CULTURE: In cooler maritime climates, plant rhododendrons in full sun to partial shade. Give more protection from the sun in warmer areas. The soil for all rhododendrons should be well enriched and on the acidic side, typical of the unamended soils along the western slope of the Cascades. Rhododendrons may survive in periods of summer drought but do not thrive under these conditions; supplemental summer water is usually compulsory to avoid the typical distressed curling of leaves.

YEAR-ROUND INTEREST: Surprisingly, there are many good rhododendrons with distinctive foliage that can be admired long after the blossoms have faded, although none of them are found among the early blossomers. Inspect the foliage of any hybrid or species you purchase to see if it has an undercoating of indumentum, which has character by itself. *Rhododendron bureavii*, R. *yakushimanum*, and many others have this remarkable woolly covering beneath their leaves in brown, red, or white, depending upon the species. Indumentum provides ornament enough to carry the shrubs through their season out of flower.

PLANT COMBINATIONS: Rhododendrons have been both overused and abused for generations in Pacific Northwest landscapes. However, by investing some thought in our choices, we can easily achieve color combinations that are subtle and soothing rather than simply dazzling or even garish. Use the early-blossoming rhododendrons to create simple and elegant scenes with other winter plants. Try *Rhododendron dauricum* with the soft yellow of *Corylopsis pauciflora* and the purple red of a dark Lenten rose. Or, perhaps, combine R. 'Olive' with the greenish yellow of *Helleborus argutifolius* below and *Stachyurus praecox* rising above.

Ribes (Currant)

Collectively known as the currants or gooseberries, the genus **Ribes** is a varied and ornamental grouping of plants well represented in the flora of the Pacific Northwest. *Ribes sanguineum*, the red-flowering currant, is perhaps our most celebrated native shrub, greatly appreciated by gardeners around the world. Narrowly upright shrubs to 8 feet in height produce showy drooping racemes of flowers in shades of deep red through purest white.

Several cultivars are grown for their exceptionally intense red flowers, including **'King Edward VII'**, **'Pulborough Scarlet'**, and **'Elk River Red'**. The color intensity seems more dependent on site conditions than on genetic propensity. Selected by Heronswood Nursery are two good pink seedlings: **'Apple Blossom'**, producing soft pink flowers —deeper colored in bud—and **'Emerson'** (after my longtime canine companion), with blossoms of rich pinkish red. **'White Icicle'** and **'Henry Henneman'** are two popular selections grown for their pure white flowers.

Of gentler effect is an Asiatic currant that thrives in semishaded areas. *Ribes laurifolium* is an evergreen species with handsome red stems and gray-green leaves. The male form has consistently larger flowers. Very hardy, it takes all that winter can muster, while still producing soft yellow flowers on drooping spikes along stems that never rise above 3 feet.

CULTURE: Grow currants in well-drained soil, in full sun to partial shade. Although they establish more quickly with summer water, currants are very drought-tolerant and should never require supplemental irrigation.

YEAR-ROUND INTEREST: Small, powdery blue fruits ripen in late summer on the native species, *Ribes sanguineum*. Both sexes are needed for fruit on *R. laurifolium*.

PLANT COMBINATIONS: The pastel yellow flowers of *Ribes laurifolium* blossom just as the color is showing on the first flowers of the hellebores. A dark pink Lenten rose is smashing in combination. All color variants of Northwest *R. sanguineum* work well together to make a pleasing blend of similar values. However, individually you can use them to enhance any one color scheme. *R.* 'Henry Henneman', for example, is striking when rising amidst a solid stand of dark green *Euphorbia amygdaloides* var. *robbiae*. R. 'Pulborough Scarlet' with the snaking stems of *Rubus tricolor* underfoot is also quite effective.

Sarcococca (Winter box)

The genus **Sarcococca** is composed of several species of diminutive evergreen shrubs that are well suited to the maritime climate. In fact, few plants measure up to the many species of winter box for sturdy and handsome evergreen ground covers used in shade. Most notably, they offer a bounty of extremely fragrant flowers in the depths of winter.

Two species are strikingly similar in appearance but, over time, develop their individual traits of identification. *Sarcococca ruscifolia* produces dense stands of 3-foot stems clothed in narrow blackish green leaves. Beginning in late January, small, spidery, perfumed blossoms of white emerge from bright green buds held in the leaf axils. Differing in its clumping nature, **S. confusa** sports broader leaves and less-undulated leaf margins. Because this species will not spread by rhizomes, set the plants close together if you want a solid ground cover.

Distinctive in its reddish purple blushed stems and gray-green leaves is *Sarcococca hookeriana* var. *digyna*. The flowers of this species, which appear throughout late January and February, are the most fragrant of the genus. It is among the best to include in our gardens, yet it is hard to find in the nursery trade. More readily available is **S. hookeriana var. humilis**, with glossy linear foliage of medium green on compact stems, forming an impenetrable ground cover to less than a foot in height. Fragrant flowers in February and March make it delightful for shaded positions on the north side of the house.

Sarcoccoca orientalis remains my favorite of this genus for flower effect alone. Although it is not quite as fragrant as S. *hookeriana* var. *digyna*, hints of its presence make their way on January and February breezes far downwind from its location in the garden. The flowers are large for the genus, with a blush of pink to the swelling buds and just-opened florets nestled amongst relatively large and broad, leathery green foliage.

CULTURE: All the *Sarcococca* species need a shaded and cool position in the woodland, with adequate moisture. Once established, they tolerate considerable drought, but avoid siting them in full sun to prevent scorched and forlorn-looking plants.

YEAR-ROUND INTEREST: Lush evergreen foliage is held handsome and intact throughout the year. Berries, which are poisonous, ripen to glossy black or reddish black, depending upon the species, from late summer through autumn.

PLANT COMBINATIONS: The dark green foliage combines well with the bright silvery foliage of many variegated woodland plants, including *Lamium, Lamiastrum,* and *Pulmonaria.*

Skimmia japonica

Ubiquitous in the maritime Northwest are plantings of **Skimmia japonica,** grown most commonly for the brilliant red or white fruit on the female plants. This evergreen shrub, growing to 3 feet, deserves more attention as an extremely fragrant and colorful species for the late-winter garden. The selected male cultivar known as **'Rubella'** presents large conical clusters of deep red buds throughout the winter months, opening in late spring to fragrant white-blushed-pink blossoms.

CULTURE: *Skimmia* requires a shaded and moist condition. It often looks quite ragged and distressed when sited in too much sun or after enduring too little moisture. The continual absence of moisture on the foliage creates the perfect environment for the skimmia mite, which ravages the leaves, leaving them spotted and discolored. Overhead supplemental irrigation helps hold mite infestation in check, but providing shade is the best solution.

YEAR-ROUND INTEREST: Female plants, with a pollinator nearby, produce bright red berries held throughout the winter. The dark green and handsome foliage of both sexes is a valuable additon to the garden throughout the year.

PLANT COMBINATIONS: Plant with yellow winter-flowering shrubs such as *Mahonia* or *Corylopsis* to provide a wonderful contrast in color and shape.

Stachyurus

Stachyurus praecox, a large, multistemmed shrub to 20 feet, produces multitudes of 6-inch, rigid, drooping flowers in February and March. The jewel-like blossoms of soft yellow coat mahogany branchlets, creating a dazzling effect, especially when highlighted by the rays of sun still low in the winter sky (see Chapter 3, "Bark"). **S. chinensis** extends the season of this genus, which begins to blossom just as S. *praecox* starts to fade in mid-March.

CULTURE: *Stachyurus* benefits from a moist cool soil yet survives without supplemental summer water when established. Give it open conditions and ample room to become a wide-spreading shrub. Prune from the base, rather than shearing it.

YEAR-ROUND INTEREST: Extending its season of interest into late spring through summer is *Stachyurus praecox* 'Aureomarginata'. The leaves of this cultivar are boldly emarginated with gold, brightening the semishaded conditions that it most prefers.

PLANT COMBINATIONS: Site most effectively to catch the sun through the drooping flowers that are produced in mid- to late winter. Consider planting it next to *Acer griseum*, the paperbark maple; the paperbark's flaky cinnamon-brown bark contrasts perfectly with the pastel yellow flowers of *Stachyurus*.

Sycopsis and × *Sycoparrotia*

Soft orange clusters of witch hazel–like blossoms, composed mostly of a central boss of orange stamens, are produced along the branches of *Sycopsis sinensis* in late winter. The contrast between these spidery flowers and the leathery evergreen foliage of this slender, small tree is quite remarkable and vastly different from the deciduous members of this family. Now most frequently encountered in Northwest arboreta and botanical gardens, *S. sinensis* deserves more attention in our home landscapes.

An interesting bigeneric hybrid between the above *Sycopsis* and *Parrotia persica* (see Chapter 3, "Bark"), known as × *Sycoparrotia semidecidua*, takes the middle road, as its name indicates, in its approach of retaining or dropping its foliage in autumn. In cold winters, it will drop all its foliage; in other winters it retains most. The flowers of this botanical mule are similar in appearance to those of its evergreen parent yet somewhat more subtle in color, with the softest touch of orange to its stamens. This multistemmed large shrub grows to 25 feet. It is a distinctive and ususual hardy shrub for inclusion in your year-round garden.

CULTURE: Cultivate *Sycopsis* and × *Sycoparrotia* in semishaded conditions, with little or no supplemental water during the summer months after establishment.

YEAR-ROUND INTEREST: The rich blackish green foliage of *Sycopsis* remains attached throughout the year. Both species add effect from foliage during the summer months.

PLANT COMBINATIONS: The dark green foliage is ideal as a backdrop to many of the lighter-blossomed winter and spring shrubs, such as yellow-flowered witch hazels and *Corylopsis*.

Viburnum (Viburnum)

Though I have been jaded by over a decade of winter horticultural gifts in the mild Northwest climate, I am still thankful for my first encounter with species of the winter-flowering **Viburnum**. When I chanced upon **V. farreri**, with white flowers that were both fresh and fragrant, the dreary midwinter weather gave no hints of breaking. This was the hope of spring incarnate, and my spirits were lifted. My appreciation for these species remains undiminished.

The most commonly available of the winter-bloomers is **Viburnum × bodnantense**. The cultivar **'Dawn'**, a rich pink, is the one most frequently encountered, although I am partial to **'Deben'**, a clean white, which more closely resembles its parents. In a mild year, *V. × bodnantense* is often in full blossom by Christmas, and can produce smatterings of flowers throughout summer and autumn. It makes a stiff arching shrub to 10 feet tall, ideal for an entry planting where you can admire the flowers during the "indoor" months.

Viburnum farreri and **V. grandiflorum** are similar in appearance to *V. bodnantense*, with fragrant white and pink flower clusters respectively. They are infrequently encountered in nurseries, but you can locate them through some retail mail-order establishments and arboreta. **V. farreri 'Nanum'** is a charming plant that remains a dense compact shrub to 3 feet. It flowers in midwinter with soft pink-blushed and fragrant blossoms.

CULTURE: The deciduous winter-flowering viburnums develop a graceful habit if you always cut entire stems at ground level when pruning, and provide adequate space for them to grow. Plant in full sun to partial shade, in soil that provides a moderate amount of moisture throughout the growing season.

YEAR-ROUND INTEREST: Other than their occasional flowers produced throughout summer and autumn, the deciduous winter-flowering viburnums offer little.

PLANT COMBINATIONS: Integrate into the mixed border or foundation planting. The soft pink and white flowers of these selections combine effectively with early-blossoming plants of similar color value— *Helleborus, Corylopsis, Mahonia,* and *Hamamelis* (witch hazel). Their stiff upright stance provides ideal scaffolding for vines in summer.

PERENNIALS

Interesting effects in Northwest gardens during late winter do not come from woody plants alone, but from the herbaceous and bulbous component of our landscapes as well. To the delight of the gardener, most herbaceous woodland plants and bulbs are destined to complete their season of blossom before a canopy of foliage forms overhead from deciduous trees or nearby grasses. These plants spring forth early, providing a dash of color to pacify the gardener until the doors of spring are thrown fully open.

Cyclamen (Cyclamen)

The genus *Cyclamen* favors the climate of the maritime Northwest and can provide, with mindful selection, twelve months of continual color. The florists' cyclamen, C. *persicum*, with imposing silver-mottled leaves and gigantic, flared flowers held on 8-inch stems, is sadly tender in our climate. However, more diminutive versions with considerably more charm offer the garden similar attributes. By far the most commonly encountered in our gardens is C. *hederifolium*. The returning rains of autumn call forth the delicate flowering stems, which spring from the earth in shades of deep rose through pure white. As flowering finishes, the stems curiously coil to withdraw the plumping packet of seeds that will mature, protected under a now-emerging clump of 3-inch succulent, dark green leaves etched in swirlings of pewter.

In early January, the magenta-to-pink flowers of another species, *Cyclamen coum*, appear from the barren floor of the woodland and are soon joined by distinctively round and marbled leaves that are among the most lovely in the genus. This species easily naturalizes in semi-shaded stands of unmown winter grass.

CULTURE: The hardy cyclamen are easily cultivated, and naturalize eagerly throughout the garden by self-sown seedlings. A rich humusy soil is beneficial, although summer dryness is a problem that this care-free genus overcomes by simply going dormant. If left undisturbed, individual plants produce huge, round, flattened tubers that generate scores of flowers.

YEAR-ROUND INTEREST: Throughout the winter months, the lovely foliage of *Cyclamen hederifolium* adorns the woodland garden in variation infrequently seen in any plant species. The lovely marbled and etched foliage of each species is a delightful element greatly appreciated during their season out of flower.

PLANT COMBINATIONS: Interplant the autumn- and winter-blossoming species with trilliums or *Eranthis hyemalis* (winter aconite), as well as with crocus that bloom in February and March.

Hacquetia epipactis

Starting as early as mid-December, bright yellow flowers surrounded by brilliant green bracts emerge on short stems of **Hacquetia epipactis**. I begin looking for the first flower buds as early as Thanksgiving and hope for blossoms by Christmas; the flowers are produced through March. This relatively unknown plant deserves more attention as a lovely, early-winter-blossoming herb for the maritime Northwest.

CULTURE: Rather carefree in semishade or full sun, *Hacquetia* needs sufficient water during the growing season for more robust establishment. Once established, it tolerates some dryness.

YEAR-ROUND INTEREST: In summer, dark green foliage produces a leafy mound to 15 inches in height, in contrast to its compactness during the blossoming season.

PLANT COMBINATIONS: The acid green and yellow stars can be enjoyed in the semishaded rock garden or the front of the herbaceous border, adding an intense jolt of color early in the season, long before most garden plants are stirring. Consider putting with the early-blossoming blue *Chionodoxa* or *Crocus* species for good contrast or, for complement, near the emerging brilliant yellow blades of Bowles' golden grass, *Milium effusum* 'Aureum'.

Iris unguicularis (Winter iris)

The delightful winter-blossoming **Iris unguicularis** is a handsome plant for both its upright evergreen swords of foliage and the surprisingly lovely blue flowers found nestled amongst the leaves from December through March. Be patient; it is extremely slow to establish from divisions, and may not present its first blossoms for two or three growing seasons after planting.

CULTURE: This species is perfectly happy baking under the southern eaves of a house, but also thrives in semishady locations that do not receive summer irrigation.

YEAR-ROUND INTEREST: Erect evergreen swords of foliage are held throughout the year.

PLANT COMBINATIONS: Especially striking with the brighter-colored forms of *Cyclamen coum*; they blossom together from early January through mid-March. As with other iris species, the upright foliage provides vertical contrast to countless more horizontal plants.

Lathyrus vernus (Spring vetchling)

Lathyrus vernus, the spring vetchling, blossoms in very early spring, offering a bejeweled combination of blue and magenta pealike flowers in late winter, among leafy clumps of foliage to 15 inches. The display from this small-tufted and polite perennial continues unchecked until early summer.

Omphalodes

Similar in culture to *Lathyrus* is the genus **Omphalodes**, represented in Northwest gardens by two species that have similar starlike forget-me-not-like flowers of lavender blue. *Omphalodes verna* differs from O. *cappadocica* by its prostrate and snaky growth habit and its somewhat less showy disposition; however, both are cheery additions to the late-winter woodland.

Parochetus communis

Parochetus communis, a leguminous ground cover whose foliage is strikingly similar to that of shamrock, pierces the monotony of the season with brilliant blue flowers of exceptional quality. It slowly colonizes stretches of shaded ground and provides handsome foliage throughout the year, although heavy snow will often spoil the effect until growth resumes the following spring.

Pulmonaria

Pulmonaria angustifolia produces a month of intensely blue blossoms, from mid-March to mid-April. This diminutive species of lungwort, with felted green leaves, is more than content to relinquish its space in the summer garden to adjacent, ramping perennials, as long as sufficient late winter sun is available to feed the emerging foliage. It combines remarkably well with early yellow-blossoming narcissus, and is also delightful at the base of *Corylopsis pauciflora* in the woodland.

Pulmonaria rubra 'Bowles Form' sends forth six weeks of rich salmon pink flowers from a tuft of lime green foliage, beginning in mid-February. It is earlier than the many good cultivars of **P.** *saccharata*, which are grown as much for the pewter-spotted summer leaves as for the stems of blue-fading-to-pink flowers produced in early spring.

CULTURE: All of these woodland herbs are easily grown in average, well-draining soil with a moderate amount of light and seasonal rains.

YEAR-ROUND INTEREST: Woodland herbaceous plants generally have only a single season of interest, and happily slip back into dormancy if supplemental summer irrigation is not provided. They enable the gardener to use the same space for plants that come to life somewhat later, filling the void left by early-blossoming components.

PLANT COMBINATIONS: The early-blossoming woody shrubs and trees provide a seasonal surplus of yellow flowers that pair superbly with the many herbaceous plants in shades of blue described above.

VINES

Clematis (Clematis)

Two species of **Clematis**, one rare and one common in cultivation, are representative of the few vines that, in flower, are ornamental in winter. *Clematis armandii* is the better known of the two. It excels in ornamental merit, but its lack of hardiness prevents it from being the vining mainstay that is implied by its overall availability. The evergreen and glossy foliage of this Chinese species is a lovely wintertime component to the vine arbor or on shrubs through which it scrambles. In late February or early March, large trusses of fragrant ivory flowers are produced in quantity on stems that may reach 25 feet in length. In cold winters, however, this vine is often killed to the ground, or the foliage becomes brown and tattered.

Clematis cirrhosa, with its finely cut and resplendent ferny foliage, is native to the Mediterranean region. From January to March, this evergreen presents 1- to 2-inch-wide blossoms with creamy white petals bespeckled with lavender. In uncommonly cold winters it loses its flowers, but generally seems hardier than C. *armandii*.

CULTURE: Both species are native to drier climates and desire a well-drained, warm location, although *Clematis armandii* flourishes in partially shaded conditions. Provide a cool and moist root run by mulching or planting a taller ground cover, such as *Epimedium*, *Vancouveria*, or *Euphorbia amygdaloides* var. *robbiae*.

YEAR-ROUND INTEREST: Foliage remains throughout the year—leathery green on *Clematis armandii*, more finely textured on C. *cirrhosa*.

Colorful Cornucopia: Berries

CHAPTER 6

Long after the last leaf falls, when rains return and frost feeds on the garden, the fruiting trees, shrubs, vines, and herbaceous perennials remain effective in the landscape. Gardens barter for feathered delivery of seeds enclosed in brightly translucent fruit by offering sweet or protein-rich edibles to their carriers. Indeed, one of the best reasons for including berrying species is the increased numbers of birds they bring to the winter garden.

Some berrying plants are self-fruitful—that is, they do not require pollen from another plant to successfully produce fruit. With others, you may need to plant at least two individuals of the same species to enhance fruit production. These individuals must be genetically different because obviously, two plants raised from cuttings of a single plant are, in genetic terms, the identical plant.

Ask knowledgeable sales staff at reputable nurseries to recommend pollinators for the berrying plants you plan to purchase. Sexed plants (male or female clones) are sometimes offered for sale, but in some instances you must take your chances on unsexed seedlings, with the hope of getting a matched set.

TREES AND SHRUBS

Berberis (Barberry)

For effects of winter fruit, their translucent shades of red make me partial to deciduous species of barberries, the genus *Berberis parvifolia* ranks top among those grown for this effect. Admire the rich reds and oranges of the dying leaves during the Christmas holidays. After the late leaf drop, however, this 4-foot shrub continues to perform, with a multitude of red berries held in clusters on its beige-colored, thorned stems.

62

Similar fruit effects are found in **Berberis wilsoniae**, a compact and rounded species to 3 feet tall, with lovely blue-green foliage throughout the summer. The fruit ripens several weeks earlier than that of B. *parvifolia*. **Berberis jamesiana** is another outstanding species, with tall, arching canes that produce enormous clusters of red, drooping fruit that shine when highlighted by the sun. The only pitfall of cultivating this species is its large size, making it adaptable only to more expansive sites.

CULTURE: Plant barberries in full sun in well-drained soils. Allow plenty of growing room to prevent the thorned stems from reaching into pathways. Cut the shrubs to ground level every third or fourth year to renew the beauty of the stems. (Fruit will be sacrificed for one season.)

YEAR-ROUND INTEREST: Look to this genus for multiple seasons of interest in your garden. Many species produce yellow to yellow-orange flowers during late winter and early spring. Autumn coloration of the deciduous species is among the best of all deciduous plants for rich swirlings of orange, red, and yellow.

PLANT COMBINATIONS: Easily integrate barberries into the mixed border with herbaceous perennials, or among foundation plantings with other deciduous and evergreen shrubs. The drooping, dark green branches of *Tsuga canadensis* 'Pendula' beautifully complement barberry's arching, sandy-colored stems.

Callicarpa (Beautyberry)

In late autumn, the genus **Callicarpa**, beautyberry, provides a display of rich lavender berries in shades infrequently encountered in the plant kingdom. Six-foot stems are studded with crops of small, light purple fruit that seems more a result of imaginative children at play than a product of nature.

Callicarpa bodinieri var. giraldii is probably the most satisfactory for the maritime Northwest and is most often encountered in nurseries as a self-fruitful cultivar known as **'Profusion'**. Also consider **C. dichotoma**, **C. japonica**, and **C. mollis**. All perform well, with nearly identical berry color. The white-berried cultivars of each species, often available in nurseries, combine quite effectively with the typical lavender forms.

CULTURE: Grow in full sun or light shade, with soil of moderate moisture content.

YEAR-ROUND INTEREST: The leaves have a brief but lovely autumn coloration of pink and purple, in some years (see this book's cover).

PLANT COMBINATIONS: Because of their limited season of interest, assign beautyberries to be "seen but not heard" in the garden—that is, let them augment any bed rather than be the focal planting. The typical lavender-berried forms come alive when planted near yellow-foliaged shrubs, such as variegated evergreen hollies or *Elaeagnus* × *ebbiginii* 'Gilt Edge'. Golden-berried selections of *Pyracantha*, *Stranvaesia*, and *Cotoneaster* also make remarkable companion plants.

Cotoneaster (Cotoneaster)

Cotoneaster species, both deciduous and evergreen, bring multiple seasons of interest to the garden. Here is a sampling of the species that offer copious fruit production as well as multiseasonal appeal.

Cotoneaster bullatus, the Peking cotoneaster, is a large, arching deciduous shrub found in many older public plantings of the Northwest. The large, dark green leaves turn handsome shades of orange and red in autumn before dropping to expose the enormous crops of fruit—each a large blood-red droplet. This now infrequently available species is exceptional for the graceful form it assumes when weighted in berry. Few weeping trees can compare with this specimen's autumnal grace if it is trained on a single stem.

The Parneyi cotoneaster, *Cotoneaster lacteus*, merits attention for both fruit and foliage. Relatively large, medium green leaves grace elegant, mahogany-colored branches to 12 feet tall. Following the milky display of flowers in early summer are numerous large clusters of small red fruit, which effectively contrast with the rich foliage. Parneyi cotoneaster responds nicely when espaliered on a southern wall. It may benefit from the added heat of this location during cold winters, as this species approaches that boundary of hardiness that separates thriving plants from the compost pile. Many consider **C. 'Cornubia'** to be among the finest of the fruiting cotoneasters. It is larger in stature than many of the other species, so use it as an effective alternative to *C. lacteus* in cold areas.

Perhaps the most beautiful in form of the evergreen species is **Cotoneaster × 'Hybridus Pendulus'**. Although it is useful as a ground-covering shrub, I suggest displaying it in an upright fashion. When heavy in large, red-orange fruit, it easily competes, along with *C. bullatus*, among the most beautiful of weeping trees. This is an ideal choice for both container plantings and foundation beds where height must be controlled.

The variation of yellow-gold fruit is wonderfully and consistently produced in **Cotoneaster** × **'Rothchildianus'**. This vigorous grower bears deep green leaves on upright yellow-green canes. Crops of rich yellow fruit mature in late autumn.

CULTURE: Cotoneasters are sun-lovers. They thrive in situations of average moisture but tolerate summer dryness once established. Pollinators are self-fruitful. To shape or contain, prune from the base of each branch rather than making heading cuts from the tip.

YEAR-ROUND INTEREST: Starry white-blushed-pink flowers in spring, handsome summer foliage, strong autumn tints among some species, and consistent large sets of fruit are all attributes owned by this genus.

PLANT COMBINATIONS: The red- or orange-berried cotoneasters are effective interplanted with golden-foliaged conifers such as *Juniperus chinensis* 'Pfitzeriana Old Gold', *Cryptomeria japonica* 'Sekkan', or *Chamaecyparis obtusa* 'Crippsii'. Yellow-fruited forms are delightful when combined with the standard, more frequently encountered red and orange berry colors.

Euonymus europaeus (Spindletree)

Several species, collectively dubbed the spindletrees, are among the finest multistemmed fruiting tall shrubs or small trees, and bear large crops of magical fruit in late autumn. The wood of **Euonymus europaeus** was once used in Europe to make spindles, hence the common name. Its long-lasting red capsules open to expose orange seeds. Several good cultivars of this species have been selected for heavier fruiting, including **'Red Cascade'** and **'Red Ace'**.

CULTURE: Have at least two individuals present to augment the fruit set of this shrub. *Euonymus* performs equally well in semishade or in full sun. It benefits from light summer watering when young, although it is apparently quite drought-tolerant when established.

YEAR-ROUND INTEREST: The autumn spectacle is among the showiest displayed by any fruiting plant.

PLANT COMBINATIONS: Although it works well in small groupings, you can integrate *Euonymus* singly into the mixed border. The fruit is displayed quite effectively in late autumn when placed near tall, late-blossoming blue and purple asters.

Idesia polycarpa

Few trees are grown in our climate for the ornamental effects of fruit alone, yet an exceptional beauty that deserves more attention is **Idesia polycarpa**. This deciduous tree of tropical demeanor, with large papery green leaves, is a rapid grower in our climate, becoming 40 feet or taller. When the soft yellow leaves fall from the branches, large foot-long dangling clusters of brilliant orange fruit, on female specimens, are just ripening. Horizontal tiers of wide-spreading branches make an imposing winter scene. This Chinese tree is rare in cultivation in the West, perhaps because it takes several years to attain fruiting age, and only unsexed plants are currently available.

CULTURE: *Idesia* flourishes in full sun to partial shade, and thrives in most soil types with a moderate amount of moisture.

YEAR-ROUND INTEREST: Large heart-shaped summer leaves turn yellow in autumn.

PLANT COMBINATIONS: Plant with bold-leaved shrubs, trees, and perennials for a powerful effect. The windmill palm, *Trachycarpus fortunei*, can add interest to the planting during the winter months and combines effectively in summer. *Acanthus mollis*, bear's breech, works nicely as a prominent semievergreen ground cover at its base.

Ilex (Holly)

Because of its popularity in wreaths and arrangements during winter holidays, the English holly, **Ilex aquifolium**, with its strong, red fruit, is often included in our gardens. Indeed, on a blustery winter's day, when gazing upon its black-green foliage and stems burdened with red fruit, I momentarily forget the climatic onslaught and marvel in its splendor. Fortunately, there are numerous more appropriate choices of evergreen fruiting hollies for our smaller gardens than the standard species, which reaches gigantic proportions in the Pacific Northwest. I recommend four of my favorites below.

Ilex aquifolium 'Bacciflava', a yellow-fruited selection of the English holly, remains more manageable in size and delivers a soft and muted effect from its fruit throughout the winter. It reaches 20 feet in height.

Ilex pedunculosa, the long-stemmed holly, is tough and durable, with nonspiny leaves and, on female plants, large dangling "earrings" of red fruit held throughout winter. This choice—although underused—large shrub grows to 15 feet.

Ilex 'September Gem' makes a dense, dark green hedge with its slightly spiny leaves. The large crops of fruit ripen early in the season, then continue performing for many months. This top-notch small hedging plant, maturing at 10 feet, has textural, sharp-toothed leaves that provide effective traffic control.

Ilex crenata 'Ivory Towers' forms an upright shrub to 4 feet, with finely textured foliage. Tiny, jewel-like greenish white berries that encrust the stems carry the garden in winter.

CULTURE: Each species of evergreen holly requires an appropriate pollinator nearby for fruit effect.

YEAR-ROUND INTEREST: Enjoy the handsome evergreen foliage provided by hollies at all times.

PLANT COMBINATIONS: The red-berried hollies are best shown among rich foliage of greens and dark blues provided by the countless conifers that thrive in our climate. The yellow-berried forms complement yellow-foliaged cultivars of conifers and broad-leaved evergreens. *Lonicera nitida* 'Baggeson's Gold', for example, works nicely in combination with *Ilex crenata* 'Ivory Towers'.

Ilex verticillata, a deciduous holly that hails from the swamps and bogs of eastern North America, is among the most effective ornamental berrying shrubs for permanently wet conditions, providing a foggy red haze of fruit throughout late autumn and early winter. Cultivars, including 'Winter Red', 'Shaver', 'Bonfire', 'Sparkleberry', and 'Sunset', are all fine and dependable fruiting female selections of this species. The plump orange-red berries are closely attached to the upright 8-inch stems, in some cases so profusely as to completely hide the bark. Because birds love the fruit, the striking effect of the berries may be short-lived.

CULTURE: A warm and sunny situation with average-to-moist soil best serves the deciduous hollies. Nonberrying male plants must be present in order for fruit to form; ask your nursery for appropriate pollinators.

YEAR-ROUND INTEREST: Dark green foliage provides some ornamental interest in summer.

PLANT COMBINATIONS: Consider using the shrubby dogwoods (see Chapter 3, "Bark") as ideal companions that have the same cultural requirements and provide complementing or contrasting effects from bark. A dark backdrop of conifers also highlights fruit effects.

Iris foetidissima (Gladwyn iris)

The Gladwin iris, *Iris foetidissima*, is a superior evergreen perennial that takes the challenges of dry shade in stride. Not grown primarily for its rather insipid lavender or yellowish flowers produced in early summer, it reserves your attention for the immense crops of orange berries that spill from its globose seed capsules from late fall into early winter.

CULTURE: Successful in either full sun with ample moisture or considerable shade and dryness, it is a welcome component in the barren difficult beds surrounding the larger conifers in Northwest woodlands.

YEAR-ROUND INTEREST: Upright glossy swords of foliage remain effective throughout the year and are the perfect framework for presentation of the remarkable fruit.

PLANT COMBINATIONS: In sunnier situations, late-blossoming asters in hues of purple combine remarkably well with the fruit of this species. Another nice contrast is with the dense, rounded domes of Miss Robb's spurge, *Euphorbia amgydaloides* var. *robbiae*, which shares its ability to thrive in dry shade.

Pernettya mucronata (Pernettya)

A genus of evergreen shrubs known as **Pernettya** is found natively in South America, New Zealand, and Tasmania, although many species thrive in the maritime Northwest. The most commonly available is **P. mucronata**, with small, dark green, needlelike leaves densely covering upright stems of cherry red. In late spring, bright white flowers are pervasively tucked among the foliage, yet it is not until late autumn that the resultant succulent fruit ripens to shades of red, pink, or white. This low- to medium-sized species easily gains in stature to 5 feet. Remove vigorous upright stems to easily control it as a medium-high ground-covering shrub that remains in fruit throughout the autumn and into winter. **P. mucronata** 'Thymifolia' is a male clone that produces a dwarf mound of dark green foliage, as well as serving as a pollen source for adjacent female plants.

CULTURE: All *Pernettya* species benefit from full-sun situations and acidic soils. Once established, they do not require summer water. Because individual plants may be either male or female or may have flowers of both sexes, you may not need to have more than one plant to have fruit. However, chances for a larger crop of colorful berries are enhanced if you plant both sexes.

YEAR-ROUND INTEREST: Enjoy tidy and textural evergreen foliage throughout the year and white flowers produced in spring on these remarkable plants.

PLANT COMBINATIONS: Ideal companions are other acid-loving plants, such as *Erica* (heaths) and *Calluna* (heathers), *Gaultheria*, and *Rhododendron*. *Pernettya* fruit is edible, though it imparts more of a colorful and refreshing squeeze of moisture than real taste.

Pyracantha (Firethorn)

The firethorns, genus **Pyracantha**, contain an abundance of desirable species and selections that thrive quite comfortably in the cool summers of our maritime environment. These generous and consistent bearers of fruit range in color from yellow through deep red, and the thorn-tipped branchlets quickly earn your respect, or at least trigger your caution when working near them.

Most pyracanthas show some propensity to tenderness and will be cut to the ground in hard winters. White flowers produced in late spring result in berries that ripen to varying degrees of orange-red, depending upon the cultivar.

Pyracantha angustifolia has proven to be one of the hardiest firethorns in my garden, with gray-green foliage and large crops of orange fruit in autumn. **P. coccinea 'Lalandei'** and **P. 'Teton'** are well-represented cultivars in commerce throughout the Western states. They are highly suited to growing on walls, as both informal or closely clipped espaliers. In exceptional years, the foliage is all but hidden by masses of fruit—orange-red on 'Lalandei', more yellow-orange on 'Teton'. These may remain intact well into winter, although I have found that during our infrequent snowfalls the crops are generally consumed within days by hungry flocks of robins, flickers, and varied thrushes.

Pyracantha atalantioides 'Gnome' has dense, spreading branches cloaked in deep green foliage and white flowers that transform it into a globular mound of snow. Though not technically a dwarf, it remains denser than any other available firethorn, lending itself well to informal low hedging and barrier plantings.

With rich sulphur yellow fruit, **Pyracantha 'Gold Rush'** is spectacular in autumn. Vigorous in growth, it quickly establishes to a shrub 12 feet tall and 5 feet wide.

CULTURE: Plant firethorns in well-drained soils and full sun. Once established, they need no further summer watering. All are self-fruitful.

YEAR-ROUND INTEREST: The mounds or columns of dark green foliage are exceptionally striking throughout the year. They contrast perfectly with clean white flowers that are produced in early spring. Autumn fruit persists into winter.

PLANT COMBINATIONS: Pyracanthas allow for an easy transition of color schemes within the same bed, due to their neutrality of green and white in spring and summer. A planting of late red tulips at the base of the shrub is pretty when both are in flower. Later in the fall, an adjacent planting of the dark purple aster 'Our Latest One' is a lovely contrast with the orange fruit.

Sorbus (Mountain ash)

The mountain ashes, *Sorbus* spp., not to be confused with the true ashes, are members of the rose family. European mountain ash, *Sorbus aucuparia*, with its crops of fluorescent orange fruit, is among the most frequently cultivated. However, other outstanding mountain ashes offer a multiplicity of seasonal attributes. Many species produce white or light pink fruit; all are well suited for use in the design of small, sunny urban landscapes.

Sorbus forrestii, a Chinese species, produces a small, rounded tree to 25 feet, with distinctive blue-green compound leaves during the summer months. The pinkish-white berries often remain attached well into early winter and, when seen from a distance, are sometimes mistaken for those of an early-blossoming ornamental cherry.

Sorbus hupehensis is similar in appearance to *S. forrestii* but has sea green leaves during the summer months and a variable fruit color of pure white through rich pink, held on pink stalks. **'Pink Pagoda'** is a fine cultivar selected by the University of British Columbia Botanical Garden. This 35-foot-tall, rounded tree consistently produces quantities of rich pink fruit, ripening through the autumn leaves of red and orange. The fruit persists well into the winter, long after the last leaves have fallen.

Sorbus prattii is a small tree with finely textured pinnate foliage and large crops of pure white berries. Birds seem less interested in white fruit than in pink or orange fruit, so these berries will remain attached longer into the winter.

CULTURE: Site *Sorbus* in full sun for best autumn color and fruit set. Well-drained but moderately moist soils are desirable.

YEAR-ROUND INTEREST: Pungent white blossoms in spring, handsome summer foliage, and strong autumn tints make the mountain ashes valuable year-round trees in Northwest gardens.

PLANT COMBINATIONS: Many species are ideal for lawn specimens or for integration into the mixed border. To best show off the bright fruit, plant with an ornamental-foliaged conifer, such as the intense *Chamaecyparis lawsoniana* 'Oregon Blue' or the dark green *Picea orientalis*.

Stranvaesia (Stranvaesia)

Stranvaesia species have superior bright red fruit that remains attached throughout the winter months. *S. davidiana* is found too rarely in landscapes around the Pacific Northwest. This upright evergreen shrub reaches 30 feet, with rusty red new growth in spring fading to rich green. White spring flowers produce large clusters of red fruit, ripening in midautumn and remaining attached throughout the winter. The fruit, in combination with the autumn reds of some leaves, creates a striking scene in midwinter. Although **S. davidiana var. undulata** is considered one of the lower-growing forms, plan on removing vigorous upright stems to keep this exceptional spreading ground cover to 24 inches.

Stranvaesia davidiana 'Fructo-luteo' produces large crops of soft yellow-blushed-pink fruit on a standard-sized plant. **S. davidiana 'Painter's Palette'** stays the course as far as fruit color is concerned; its clusters of bright red fruit, however, are nestled among leaves that are splashed with white, pink, and green. Although slower growing than the species, 'Painter's Palette' develops into a colorful and anchoring component of a mixed border or foundation planting, highly effective during the winter months.

CULTURE: *Stranvaesia* is best sited to full sun with well-drained soil, although it responds to supplemental moisture during the growing season. Once established, this species is moderately drought-tolerant, but the fruit set may be diminished if the plants are stressed by too much dryness. In partial shade they grow much taller and less dense.

YEAR-ROUND INTEREST: These are handsome year-round components of the maritime garden. Medium green, linear leaves, each with an undulating leaf margin, may turn brilliant shades of crimson if grown in full sun and will remain attached throughout the winter. In late spring, observe the large clusters of white flowers, which are eagerly besieged by bees.

PLANT COMBINATIONS: Use as a single specimen in the lawn or group as an informal, unsheared hedge. The brassy red fruit of the standard species contrasts beautifully with deep greens provided by conifers and broad-leaved evergreens.

VINES

I am passionately committed to the use of vines in my garden, as vertical components that, when trained to grow among shrubs and trees, often provide a second season of flower interest for a plant long out of blossom. Vines can be selected for reasons other than their flowers; some produce fruit that persists through the winter.

Lonicera (Honeysuckle)

Far more appreciated in my garden for fruit than for flower is **Lonicera alesuosmoides**. A semivigorous honeysuckle with shiny evergreen leaves, it bears yellowish flowers in early spring that are rather small and insipid. The subsequent large sets of purple-black fruit with a whitish bloom are delightful, however. This is one of the most effective hardy evergreen vines available for fruit effect alone.

Also effective for winter fruit is **Lonicera henryi**. What it lacks in individual berry size it makes up for in its highly textural green foliage. Each leaf, slightly curled under during the summer months, becomes more acutely so during the colder winter temperatures, creating an interesting and unique effect in combination with the dark blue fruit that remains attached.

CULTURE: Thriving in full sun, with adequate summer moisture, these *Lonicera* also tolerate partial shade. Though quickly covering an arbor or lattice, they will not swamp their locality like many vines do.

YEAR-ROUND INTEREST: Planted with deciduous clematis, evergreen honeysuckle foliage fills both a barren arbor and the winter void felt after the clematis foliage drops in autumn.

PLANT COMBINATIONS: Consider growing deciduous clematis through evergreen *Lonicera* vines. *Clematis* 'Duchess of Edinburgh' all but disappears in the tangle of foliage from the honeysuckle in my garden yet enlivens the scene when its large, double flowers of rose white appear, nestled amongst dark evergreen foliage.

Appendixes

Plant Characteristics *(Tables)*

    Bark Effects in the Winter Garden   *74*

    Foliage Effects in the Winter Garden   *78*

    Flower Effects in the Winter Garden   *82*

    Berry Effects in the Winter Garden   *88*

    Fragrance in the Winter Garden   *92*

Public Winter Gardens   *94*

Plant Buying Directory   *96*

Bibliography   *98*

Index   *101*

Bark Effects in the Winter Garden

Plant Name	Plant Type	Color	Season of Interest
Acer davidii	decid. tree	white and green stripes	year-round
A. griseum	decid. tree	rich brown-copper	year-round
A. pensylvanicum	decid. tree	white and green stripes	year-round
A. pensylvanicum 'Erythrocladum'	decid. tree	brilliant red young twigs	year-round
A. rufinerve	decid. tree	white and green stripes	year-round
A. tegmentosum	decid. tree	white and green stripes	year-round
Arbutus × andrachnoides	ever. tree	brilliant greenish white	year-round
A. 'Marina'	ever. tree	copper-brown	year-round
A. menziesii	ever. tree	flaky brown	year-round
Arctostaphylos canescens	ever. shrub	rich brown-copper	year-round
A. columbiana	ever. shrub	rich brown-copper	year-round
A. manzanita	ever. shrub	rich brown-copper	year-round
Betula albo-sinensis var. septentrionalis	decid. tree	pinkish white	year-round
B. apoiensis	decid. shrub	copper	year-round
B. jacquemontii	decid. tree	white	year-round
B. nana	decid. shrub	copper	year-round
B. nigra	decid. tree	flaky brownish white	year-round
B. nigra 'Fox River'	decid. tree	flaky brownish white	year-round
Cornus alba 'Elegantissima'	decid. shrub	red	year-round
C. alba 'Kelseyi'	decid. shrub	orange-red	year-round
C. alba 'Kesselringii'	decid. shrub	black red	year-round
C. alba 'Silver and Gold'	decid. shrub	yellow	year-round
C. alba 'Spaethii'	decid. shrub	red	year-round
C. kousa	decid. tree	mottled green, yellow, brown	year-round
C. stolonifera 'Flaviraemea'	decid. shrub	yellow	year-round
Corylus avellana 'Contorta'	decid. shrub	yellow	Feb–Mar
Lagerstroemea spp.	decid. tree	mottled in various shades	year-round

● full sun ❱ partial sun ▲ shade

Additional Features	Light	Moisture	Diseases/ Insects
autumn foliage red, orange	❱ ●	mod	aphids
autumn foliage red, orange	❱ ●	mod	aphids
autumn foliage yellow	❱ ●	mod	aphids
autumn foliage yellow	❱ ●	mod	aphids
autumn foliage red, orange	❱ ●	mod	aphids
autumn foliage yellow	❱ ●	mod	aphids
spring blossoms white, autumn fruit red	●	dry	none
autumn blossoms pink	●	dry	none
spring blossoms white, autumn fruit red	●	dry	anthracnose
spring blossoms pinkish white, autumn fruit red	●	dry	none
spring blossoms white, autumn fruit red	●	dry	none
spring blossoms pinkish white, autumn fruit red	●	dry	none
autumn foliage yellow	●	mod	aphids, birch leaf miner, birch bark borer
autumn foliage yellow	●	mod	aphids, birch leaf miner, birch bark borer
autumn foliage yellow	●	mod–moist	aphids, birch leaf miner, birch bark borer
autumn foliage yellow	●	mod–wet	aphids, birch leaf miner, birch bark borer
autumn foliage yellow	●	wet	aphids, birch leaf miner, birch bark borer
autumn foliage yellow	●	wet	aphids, birch leaf miner, birch bark borer
summer, autumn foliage white variegation, pink in autumn	●	mod–wet	none
summer foliage green	●	mod–wet	none
summer foliage green	●	mod–wet	none
summer, autumn foliage white variegation, pink in autumn	●	mod–wet	none
summer foliage yellow variegation	●	mod–wet	none
spring blossoms white, autumn foliage red, orange	❱ ●	mod	none
summer foliage green	●	mod–wet	none
silhouette	❱ ●	mod	none
late summer blossoms red, pink, white	●	mod	none

Bark Effects 75

Bark Effects (CONTINUED)

Plant Name	Plant Type	Color	Season of Interest
Metasequoia glyptostroboides	decid. tree	red-brown, highly textured	year-round
Parrotia persica	decid. shrub	mottled green and brown	year-round
Persea yunnanensis	ever. tree	black	year-round
Pinus bungeana	ever. conifer	mottled green and brown	year-round
P. densiflora	ever. conifer	cinnamon red	year-round
Prunus serrula	decid. tree	bronze	year-round
Pseudocydonia sinensis	decid. tree	mottled	year-round
Salix alba 'Britzensis'	decid. tree	brilliant orange	Nov–Apr
S. alba var. *vitellina*	decid. tree	yellow	Nov–Apr
S. gracilistyla	decid. tree	white	Nov–Apr
S. purpurea 'Nana'	decid. shrub	soft purple	Nov–Apr
Stewartia monodelpha	decid. tree	flaky brown	year-round
S. pseudocamellia	decid. tree	mottled green, white, brown	year-round

Additional Features	Light	Moisture	Diseases/Insects
spring foliage bright green, autumn foliage red-russet	❱ ●	mod–wet	none
winter blossoms red, autumn foliage red, orange	●	dry–mod	none
foliage entire year	▲ ❱	mod	none
green needles entire year	●	mod	none
green needles entire year	●	mod	none
spring blossoms white	●	mod	brown rot
spring blossoms pink, autumn fruit large yellow quince	●	mod	none
spring blossoms silver catkins, summer foliage green	●	mod–wet	twig blight, twig borer
spring blossoms silver catkins, summer foliage green	●	mod–wet	twig blight, twig borer
spring blossoms silver catkins, summer foliage green	●	mod–wet	twig blight, twig borer
spring blossoms silver catkins, summer foliage green	●	mod–wet	twig blight, twig borer
spring blossoms white, autumn foliage red, orange	❱ ●	mod	none
spring blossoms white, autumn foliage red, orange	❱ ●	mod	none

Foliage Effects in the Winter Garden

Plant Name	Plant Type	Color	Season of Interest
Abies *procera* 'Glauca'	ever. conifer	green, blue	year-round
Berberis *calliantha*	ever. shrub	green, white beneath	year-round
B. × *gladwynensis* 'Wm. Penn'	ever. shrub	green with red	year-round
B. *julianae*	ever. shrub	green with red	year-round
B. × *stenophylla* and cultivars	ever. shrub	blue-green	year-round
Bergenia *cordifolia*	perennial	green with purple	year-round
Castanopsis *chrysophylla*	ever. tree	dark green, yellow beneath	year-round
Cedrus *atlantica* 'Glauca'	ever. conifer	blue	year-round
C. *atlantica* 'Glauca Fastigiata'	ever. conifer	blue	year-round
Chamaecyparis *lawsoniana* 'Aurea'	ever. conifer	yellow	year-round
C. *lawsoniana* 'Oregon Blue'	ever. conifer	blue	year-round
C. *lawsoniana* 'Pembury Blue'	ever. conifer	blue	year-round
C. *lawsoniana* 'Spek'	ever. conifer	blue	year-round
C. *lawsoniana* 'Stewartii'	ever. conifer	yellow	year-round
C. *obtusa* 'Gracilis'	ever. conifer	green	year-round
C. *obtusa* 'Nana Gracilis'	ever. conifer	green	year-round
Cryptomeria *japonica* 'Elegans'	ever. conifer	bronze	year-round
C. *japonica* 'Elegans Aurea'	ever. conifer	yellow	year-round
Cupressus *glabra* 'Pyramidalis'	ever. conifer	blue	year-round
Elaeagnus × *ebbiginii* 'Gilt Edge'	ever. shrub	yellow	year-round
E. *pungens*	ever. shrub	gray-green	year-round
Euphorbia *amygdaloides* var. robbiae	ever. perennial	green	year-round
Eurya *japonica*	ever. shrub	green	year-round
E. *japonica* 'Winter Wine'	ever. shrub	plum green	year-round
Ilex *aquifolium* 'Flavescens'	ever. shrub	yellow	year-round
I. *crenata* 'Convexa'	ever. shrub	green	year-round
I. 'O Spring'	ever. shrub	yellow	year-round
Juniperus *squamata* 'Blue Star'	ever. conifer	blue	year-round
Lamium *maculatum*	ever. perennial	white ('White Nancy')	year-round
Leucothoe *davisae*	ever. shrub	green	year-round
L. *fontanesiana*	ever. shrub	green	year-round
L. *fontanesiana* 'Rainbow'	ever. shrub	green, red, white	year-round
Microbiota *decussata*	ever. shrub	green, russet green	year-round

Additional Features	Light	Moisture	Diseases/ Insects
spring 'flower' buds purple	●	mod	adelgids, aphids
spring blossoms yellow	●	mod	none
spring blossoms yellow	●	mod	none
spring blossoms yellow	●	mod	none
spring blossoms yellow-orange	●	mod	none
early spring blossoms pink	❯ ●	mod	root weevils
—	●	dry–mod	none
—	●	mod	none
—	●	mod	none
—	●	mod	phytophora
—	●	mod	phytophora
—	●	mod	phytophora
—	●	mod	phytophora
—	●	mod	phytophora
—	●	mod	none
—	●	mod	none
—	●	mod	none
—	●	mod	none
—	●	dry–mod	none
autumn flowers white	❯ ●	mod	none
autumn flowers white	❯ ●	mod	none
spring blossoms chartreuse	▲ ●	dry–mod	none
spring blossoms white	❯	mod	none
spring flowers white	❯	mod	none
spring flowers white	●	mod	none
autumn fruit black	●	mod	none
spring flowers white	●	mod	none
—	●	mod	juniper twig blight
spring blossoms white	❯	dry–mod	none
spring blossoms white	❯ ●	mod–moist	none
spring blossoms white	❯	mod	none
spring blossoms white	❯	mod	none
—	▲ ❯ ●	mod	none

Foliage Effects **79**

Plant Name	Plant Type	Color	Season of Interest
Nandina domestica 'Nana'	ever. shrub	green, with winter red	year-round
Ophiopogon planiscapus	ever. perennial	black ('Nigrescens')	year-round
Osmanthus × burkwoodii	ever. shrub	green	year-round
O. decorus	ever. shrub	green	year-round
O. delavayi	ever. shrub	green	year-round
O. heterophyllus	ever. shrub	green	year-round
O. heterophyllus 'Goshiki'	ever. shrub	yellow mottled	year-round
O. heterophyllus 'Ogon'	ever. shrub	yellow	year-round
O. heterophyllus 'Purpureus'	ever. shrub	green, purple	year-round
O. heterophyllus 'Sasaba'	ever. shrub	green	year-round
O. heterophyllus 'Variegatus'	ever. shrub	yellow	year-round
Pachistima canbyi	ever. shrub	green	year-round
P. myrsinites	ever. shrub	green	year-round
Pachysandra terminalis	ever. perennial	green	year-round
P. terminalis 'Green Sheen'	ever. perennial	glossy green	year-round
P. terminalis 'Variegata'	ever. perennial	yellow	year-round
Picea omorika	ever. conifer	blue-green	year-round
P. orientalis	ever. conifer	green	year-round
Pinus sylvestris 'Aurea'	ever. conifer	yellow	year-round
Quercus glauca	ever. tree	green	year-round
Q. hypoleucoides	ever. tree	dark green, white beneath	year-round
Q. ilex	ever. tree	green	year-round
Q. myrsinifolia	ever. tree	green	year-round
Q. suber	ever. tree	green	year-round
Stranvaesia davidiana	ever. shrub	red ('Painter's Palette ')	Oct–Jan
Taxus baccata 'Standishii'	ever. conifer	yellow	year-round
Thuja plicata 'Zebrina'	ever. conifer	yellow-green	year-round
Vancouveria planipetala	ever. perennial	glossy green	year-round
Viburnum awabuki var. chindo	ever. shrub	glossy green	year-round
V. cinnamomifolium	ever. shrub	green	year-round
V. davidii	ever. shrub	green	year-round
V. × pragense	ever. shrub	glossy green	year-round
V. rhytidophyllum	ever. shrub	dull green	year-round

Additional Features	Light	Moisture	Diseases/ Insects
spring blossoms white, autumn berries red	▶ ●		none
summer flowers lavender	▶ ●	mod	none
spring blossoms white	▶ ●	mod	none
spring blossoms white	▶ ●	dry–mod	none
spring blossoms white	▶ ●	mod	none
autumn blossoms white	▶ ●	mod	none
autumn blossoms white	▶ ●	mod	none
autumn blossoms white	▶ ●	mod	none
autumn blossoms white	▶ ●	mod	none
autumn blossoms white	▶ ●	mod	none
autumn blossoms white	▶ ●	mod	none
spring blossoms red	▶ ●	dry–mod	none
spring blossoms red	▶ ●	dry–mod	none
spring blossoms white	▲ ▶	mod	none
spring blossoms white	▲ ▶	mod	none
spring blossoms white	▶	mod	none
—	●	mod	none
—	●	mod	aphids
—	●	mod	pine shoot moth
spring foliage glossy red-green	●	mod	none
—	●	dry–mod	none
—	●	dry–mod	none
—	●	mod	none
—	●	dry–mod	none
spring blossoms white, autumn fruit red	●	mod	none
—	▲ ▶	mod–moist	none
—	▶ ●	mod	none
spring blossoms white	▲ ▶	dry–mod	none
spring blossoms white	▶ ●	mod	none
winter/spring blossoms white, autumn fruit metallic blue	▶ ●	mod	none
winter/spring blossoms white, autumn fruit metallic blue	▶ ●	mod	none
spring blossoms white	▶ ●	mod	none
spring blossoms white, autumn fruit red, black	▶	mod	none

Foliage Effects 81

Flower Effects in the Winter Garden

Plant Name	Plant Type	Color	Season of Interest
Abeliophylum distichum	decid. shrub	white	Feb
A. distichum 'Roseum'	decid. shrub	pink	Feb
Azara microphylla	ever. shrub	greenish white	Mar
A. microphylla 'Variegata'	ever. shrub	greenish white	Mar
Berberis darwinii	ever. shrub	orange	Mar
B. linearifolia	ever. shrub	orange	Mar
Camellia japonica	ever. shrub	white, pink, red	Jan–Apr
C. oleifera	ever. shrub	white	Oct–Jan
C. sasanqua	ever. shrub	white, pink, red	Oct–Jan
C. sinensis	ever. shrub	white	Oct–Dec
C. × williamsii 'Donation'	ever. shrub	pink	Feb–Apr
Chimonanthus praecox	decid. shrub	yellow	Jan–Mar
C. praecox var. luteus	decid. shrub	golden yellow	Jan–Mar
Clematis armandii	ever. vine	white	Feb–Mar
C. cirrhosa	ever. vine	cream	Feb–Mar
Corylopsis glabrescens	decid. shrub	yellow	Mar–Apr
C. pauciflora	decid. shrub	yellow	Mar
C. sinensis	decid. shrub	yellow	Mar–Apr
C. spicata	decid. shrub	yellow	Mar–Apr
Cyclamen coum	bulb	white, pink, rose	Dec–Feb
C. hederifolium	bulb	white, pink, rose	Oct–Dec
C. repandum	bulb	pink	Feb–Apr
Daphne blagayana	ever. shrub	white	Feb–Mar
D. laureola	ever. shrub	green	Feb–Mar
D. laureola var. philippi	ever. shrub	green	Feb–Mar
D. mezereum	decid. shrub	purple/white	Feb
D. odora	ever. shrub	white/pink	Feb–Mar
Erica arborea var. alpina	ever. shrub	white	Mar–Apr
E. carnea 'King George'	ever. shrub	rose red	Feb–Apr
E. carnea 'Springwood'	ever. shrub	white	Feb–Apr
E. carnea 'Springwood Pink'	ever. shrub	pink	Feb–Apr
E. × darleyensis 'Darley Dale'	ever. shrub	pink	Nov–Jan
E. × darleyensis "Silberschmelze'	ever. shrub	white	Nov–Jan
E. lusitanica	ever. shrub	pinkish white	Feb–Mar

Additional Features	Light	Moisture	Diseases/Insects
winter stems black	●	mod	none
winter stems black	●	mod	none
green foliage year-round	◗ ●	mod	none
variegated foliage year-round	◗ ●	mod	none
green foliage year-round	◗ ●	mod	none
green foliage year-round	◗ ●	mod	none
green foliage year-round	◗ ●	mod	none
green foliage year-round	◗	mod	none
green foliage year-round	◗	mod	none
green foliage year-round	◗	mod	none
green foliage year-round	◗	mod	none
—	◗ ●	mod	none
—	◗ ●	mod	none
green foliage year-round	◗	mod	none
green foliage year-round	●	mod	none
autumn foliage yellow	◗ ●	mod	none
autumn foliage yellow	◗	mod	none
autumn foliage yellow	◗ ●	mod	none
autumn foliage yellow	◗ ●	mod	none
winter foliage marbled green, silver	◗	mod	none
winter foliage marbled green, silver	◗	mod	none
spring foliage marbled green	◗	mod	none
green foliage year-round	◗ ●	mod	none
summer fruit black (poisonous)	◗ ●	mod	none
tidy mound of green foliage year-round	▲ ◗	mod	none
autumn fruit red (poisonous)	●	mod	none
green foliage year-round	◗	mod	none
green foliage year-round	●	mod	none
green foliage year-round	●	mod	none
green foliage year-round	●	mod	none
green foliage year-round	●	mod	none
green foliage year-round	●	mod	none
green foliage year-round	●	mod	none
green foliage year-round	●	mod	none

Flower Effects (CONTINUED)

Plant Name	Plant Type	Color	Season of Interest
Garrya elliptica	ever. shrub	white-green	Feb
G. elliptica 'James Roof'	ever. shrub	white-green	Feb
G. × issaquahensis	ever. shrub	white-green	Feb
Hacquetia epipactis	decid. perennial	yellow	Dec–Apr
Hamamelis × intermedia 'Arnold's Promise'	decid. shrub	bright yellow	Dec–Mar
H. × intermedia 'Diane'	decid. shrub	red	Dec–Mar
H. × intermedia 'Jelena'	decid. shrub	red	Dec–Mar
H. × intermedia 'Ruby Glow'	decid. shrub	red	Dec–Mar
H. × intermedia 'Sunburst'	decid. shrub	golden yellow	Dec–Mar
H. × intermedia 'Winter Beauty'	decid. shrub	orange	Dec–Mar
H. japonica	decid. shrub	yellow	Jan–Feb
H. mollis	decid. shrub	yellow	Jan–Feb
Helleborus argutifolius	ever. perennial	green	Dec–Apr
H. foetidus	ever. perennial	green	Feb–Apr
H. niger	ever. perennial	white	Feb–Apr
H. × orientalis	ever. perennial	white, pink, red	Feb–Apr
Iris unguicularis	ever. perennial	light blue	Dec–Mar
Jasminum nudiflorum	decid. shrub	yellow	Feb
Lathyrus vernus	decid. perennial	purple-red	Feb–Mar
Lindera obtusiloba	decid. shrub	yellow	Mar
Lonicera fragrantissima	decid. shrub	white	Dec–Mar
L. × purpusii	decid. shrub	white	Dec–Mar
L. standishii	decid. shrub	white	Dec–Mar
Mahonia × 'Arthur Menzies'	ever. shrub	yellow	Dec–Feb
M. bealei	ever. shrub	yellow	Dec–Feb
M. japonica	ever. shrub	yellow	Jan–Feb
M. lomariifolia	ever. shrub	yellow	Jan–Feb
M. × media cultivars	ever. shrub	yellow	Jan–Feb
Omphalodes cappadocica	decid. perennial	blue	Mar
O. verna	decid. perennial	blue, white	Mar
Parochetus communis	semi-ever. perennial	blue	Nov–Apr

Additional Features	Light	Moisture	Diseases/ Insects
green foliage year-round, autumn purple fruit on female plants	❯ ●	mod	none
green foliage year-round	❯ ●	mod	none
green foliage year-round, autumn purple fruit on female plants	❯ ●	mod	none
summer foliage green	❯ ●	mod	none
autumn foliage yellow	❯ ●	mod	none
autumn foliage red	❯ ●	mod	none
autumn foliage orange, red	❯ ●	mod	none
autumn foliage red	❯ ●	mod	none
autumn foliage yellow	❯ ●	mod	none
autumn foliage orange, red	❯ ●	mod	none
autumn foliage yellow	❯ ●	mod	none
autumn foliage yellow	❯ ●	mod	none
green foliage year-round	❯ ●	mod	botrytis
green foliage year-round	❯	mod	botrytis
green foliage year-round	❯	mod	botrytis
green foliage year-round	❯	mod	botrytis
green foliage year-round	❯ ●	dry–mod	none
green stems year-round	❯ ●	mod	none
—	❯	mod	none
summer foliage green, autumn foliage yellow	❯	mod	none
—	❯ ●	mod	none
—	❯ ●	mod	none
—	❯ ●	mod	none
foliage year-round, summer fruit blue	❯	mod	none
foliage year-round, summer fruit blue	❯	mod	none
foliage year-round, summer fruit blue	❯	mod	none
foliage year-round, summer fruit blue	❯	mod	none
foliage year-round, summer fruit blue	❯	mod	none
summer foliage green	❯	mod	none
summer foliage green	❯	mod	none
green foliage with purple markings year-round	❯ ●	mod	none

Plant Name	Plant Type	Color	Season of Interest
Prunus mume	tree	pink	Mar
P. subhirtella 'Autumnalis Rosea'	tree	pink	Oct–Apr
P. subhirtella 'Pendula'	tree	pink	Feb–Apr
P. subhirtella 'Whitcombii'	tree	pink	Feb–Apr
Pulmonaria angustifolia	decid. perennial	blue-pink	Feb–Mar
P. rubra 'Bowles Form'	decid. perennial	pink-red	Feb–Mar
P. saccharata	decid. perennial	blue-pink	Mar
Rhododendron ciliatum	ever. shrub	pinkish white	Mar
R. 'Cilpinense'	ever. shrub	pink	Mar
R. moupinense	ever. shrub	white	Mar
R. mucronulatum	decid. shrub	lavender	Dec–Mar
R. mucronulatum 'Album'	decid. shrub	white	Dec–Mar
R. mucronulatum 'Cornell Pink'	decid. shrub	pink	Dec–Mar
R. 'Olive'	ever. shrub	pink	Feb–Mar
R. 'Praecox'	ever. shrub	lavender	Mar
R. strigillosum	ever. shrub	red	Mar
Ribes laurifolium	ever. shrub	yellow	Mar
R. sanguineum cultivars	decid. shrub	red, pink, white	Mar–Apr
Sarcococca confusa	ever. shrub	white	Jan–Feb
S. hookeriana var. *digyna*	ever. shrub	white	Jan–Feb
S. hookeriana var. *humilis*	ever. shrub	white	Jan–Feb
S. orientalis	ever. shrub	white	Jan–Feb
S. ruscifolia	ever. shrub	white	Jan–Feb
Skimmia japonica	ever. shrub	white flowers	Feb–Mar
S. japonica 'Rubella'	ever. shrub	red buds to white flowers	Nov–Apr
Stachyurus chinensis	decid. shrub	yellow	Mar–late Apr
S. praecox	decid. shrub	yellow	Feb–Apr
Sycoparrotia semidecidua	semi-evergreen shrub	orange	Mar–Apr
Sycopsis sinensis	ever. tree	orange	Feb–Mar

Additional Features	Light	Moisture	Diseases/Insects
—	●	mod	brown rot
—	●	mod	brown rot
—	●	mod	brown rot
—	●	mod	brown rot
—	▶	mod	none
—	▶	mod	none
summer foliage silver variegation	▶	mod	none
green foliage year-round	▶	mod	phytophora, root weevils
green foliage year-round	▶ ●	mod	phytophora, root weevils
green foliage year-round	▶	mod	phytophora, root weevils
autumn foliage yellow, red	▶ ●	mod	phytophora, root weevils
autumn foliage yellow	▶ ●	mod	phytophora, root weevils
autumn foliage yellow	▶ ●	mod	phytophora, root weevils
green foliage year-round	▶ ●	mod	phytophora, root weevils
green foliage year-round	▶ ●	mod	phytophora, root weevils
green foliage year-round	▶	mod	phytophora, root weevils
green foliage year-round	▶	mod	none
autumn fruit blue	▶	mod	alternate host, white pine blister rust
green foliage year-round	▲ ▶	mod	none
green foliage year-round	▲ ▶	mod	none
green foliage year-round	▲ ▶	mod	none
green foliage year-round	▲ ▶	mod	none
green foliage year-round	▲ ▶	mod	none
green foliage year-round, autumn red berries on female plants	▶	mod	none
green foliage year-round	▶	mod	spider mites
red branchlets year-round, summer fruit green	▶ ●	mod	none
red branchlets year-round, summer fruit green	▶ ●	mod	none
green foliage in mild years	▶ ●	mod	none
green foliage year-round	▶	mod	none

Flower Effects (CONTINUED)

Plant Name	Plant Type	Color	Season of Interest
Viburnum × *bodnantense* 'Dawn'	decid. shrub	pink	Jan–Mar
V. × *bodnantense* 'Deben'	decid. shrub	white	Jan–Mar
V. farreri	decid. shrub	pink	Jan–Mar
V. farreri 'Nanum'	decid. shrub	pink	Jan–Mar
V. grandiflorum	decid. shrub	white	Jan–Mar

Berry Effects in the Winter Garden

Plant Name	Plant Type	Fruit Color	Season of Interest
Berberis jamesiana	decid. shrub	red	Nov–Jan
B. parvifolia	decid. shrub	red	Nov–Jan
B. wilsoniae	decid. shrub	red	Nov–Jan
Callicarpa bodinieri var. *giraldii*	decid. shrub	lavender	Oct–Dec
C. dichotoma	decid. shrub	lavender	Oct–Dec
C. japonica	decid. shrub	lavender	Oct–Dec
C. mollis	decid. shrub	lavender	Oct–Dec
C. 'Profusion'	decid. shrub	lavender	Oct–Dec
Cotoneaster bullatus	decid. shrub	red	Nov–Jan
C. 'Cornubia'	ever. shrub	red	Nov–Jan
C. horizontalis	decid. shrub	red	Nov–Jan
C. 'Hybridus Pendulus'	ever. shrub	red	Nov–Jan
C. lacteus	ever. shrub	red	Nov–Jan
C. 'Rothschildianus'	ever. shrub	yellow	Nov–Jan
Euonymus europaeus cultivars	decid. shrub	pink and orange	Oct–Dec
E. sieboldianus	decid. shrub	pink and orange	Oct–Dec
Idesia polycarpa	decid. tree	orange	Oct–Dec

Additional Features	Light	Moisture	Diseases/ Insects
summer foliage green	▶ ●	mod	none
summer foliage green	▶ ●	mod	none
summer foliage green	▶ ●	mod	none
summer foliage green	▶ ●	mod	none
summer foliage green	▶ ●	mod	none

Additional Features	Light	Moisture	Diseases/ Insects
spring blossoms yellow, autumn foliage red, orange	●	mod	alternate host, wheat rust
spring blossoms yellow, autumn foliage red, orange	●	mod	alternate host, wheat rust
spring blossoms yellow, autumn foliage red, orange	●	mod	alternate host, wheat rust
autumn foliage pink	▶ ●	mod	none
autumn foliage pink	▶ ●	mod	none
autumn foliage pink	▶ ●	mod	none
autumn foliage pink	▶ ●	mod	none
autumn foliage pink	▶ ●	mod	none
spring blossoms white, autumn foliage red, orange	●	mod	none
spring blossoms white, green foliage year-round	●	mod	none
spring blossoms white, autumn foliage red, orange	●	mod	autumn webworm
spring blossoms white, green foliage year-round	●	mod	none
spring blossoms white, green foliage year-round	●	mod	none
spring blossoms white, green foliage year-round	●	mod	none
autumn foliage red, yellow	▶ ●	mod	none
autumn foliage red, yellow	▶ ●	mod	none
autumn foliage yellow	▶	mod	none

Flower Effects/Berry Effects **89**

Berry Effects (CONTINUED)

Plant Name	Plant Type	Fruit Color	Season of Interest
Ilex aquifolium	ever. tree	red	Oct–Feb
I. aquifolium 'Baccaflava'	ever. tree	yellow	Oct–Feb
I. crenata 'Ivory Towers'	ever. shrub	white	Oct–Feb
I. pedunculosa	ever. shrub	red	Oct–Jan
I. 'September Gem'	ever. shrub	red	Sept–Dec
I. 'Sparkleberry'	decid. shrub	red	Oct–Dec
I. verticillata and cultivars	decid. shrub	red	Oct–Dec
Iris foetidissima	ever. perennial	orange	Oct–Dec
Lonicera alesuosmoides	ever. vine	blue	Oct–Dec
L. henryi	ever. vine	blue	Oct–Dec
Pernettya mucronata	ever. shrub	red, pink, white	Oct–Dec
P. mucronata 'Thymifolia'	ever. shrub	—	Apr
Pyracantha angustifolia	ever. shrub	orange	Oct–Dec
P. atalantioides 'Gnome'	ever. shrub	orange-red	Oct–Dec
P. coccinea 'Lalandei'	ever. shrub	orange-red	Oct–Dec
P. 'Gold Rush'	ever. shrub	yellow	Oct–Dec
P. 'Teton'	ever. shrub	orange-red	Oct–Dec
Sorbus aucuparia	decid. tree	orange	Oct–Dec
S. forestii	decid. tree	white	Oct–Dec
S. hupehensis	decid. tree	white-pink	Oct–Dec
S. hupehensis 'Pink Pagoda'	decid. tree	rich pink	Oct–Dec
S. prattii	decid. tree	white	Oct–Dec
Stranvaesia davidiana	ever. shrub	red	Oct–Jan
S. davidiana 'Fructo-luteo'	ever. shrub	yellow	Oct–Jan
S. davidiana var. *undulata*	ever. shrub	red	Oct–Jan

Additional Features	Light	Moisture	Diseases/ Insects
spring blossoms white, green foliage year-round	▶ ●	mod	none
spring blossoms white, green foliage year-round	▶ ●	mod	none
spring blossoms white, green foliage year-round	●	mod	none
spring blossoms white, green foliage year-round	▶ ●	mod	none
spring blossoms white, green foliage year-round	●	mod	none
spring blossoms white	●	mod–wet	none
spring blossoms white	●	mod–wet	none
spring blossoms lavender, green foliage year-round	▲ ●	dry–mod	none
spring blossoms yellow, green foliage year-round	▶ ●	mod	none
spring blossoms red, green foliage year-round	▶ ●	mod	none
spring blossoms white, green foliage year-round	▶ ●	mod	none
dwarf male pollinator	▶ ●	mod	none
spring blossoms white, green foliage year-round	●	mod	none
spring blossoms white, green foliage year-round	●	mod	none
spring blossoms white, green foliage year-round	●	mod	none
spring blossoms white, green foliage year-round	●	mod	none
spring blossoms white, green foliage year-round	●	mod	none
spring blossoms white, autumn foliage orange, red	●	mod	none
spring blossoms white, autumn foliage orange, red	●	mod	none
spring blossoms white, autumn foliage orange, red	●	mod	none
spring blossoms white, autumn foliage orange, red	●	mod	none
spring blossoms white, autumn foliage orange, red	●	mod	none
spring blossoms white, green foliage year-round	●	mod	none
spring blossoms white; green, red, white foliage year-round	●	mod	none
spring blossoms white, green foliage year-round	●	mod	none

Fragrance in the Winter Garden

Plant Name	Plant Type	Color	Season of Interest
Abeliophyllum *distichum*	decid. shrub	white	Feb
A. distichum 'Roseum'	decid. shrub	pink	Feb
Azara *microphylla*	ever. shrub	greenish white	Mar
A. microphylla 'Variegata'	ever. shrub	greenish white	Mar
Camellia *oleifera*	ever. shrub	white	Oct–Jan
C. sasanqua	ever. shrub	white, pink, red	Oct–Jan
C. sinensis	ever. shrub	white	Oct–Dec
Chimonanthus *praecox*	decid. shrub	yellow	Jan–Mar
Clematis *armandii*	ever. vine	white	Feb–Mar
Daphne *laureola*	ever. shrub	green	Feb–Mar
D. mezereum	decid. shrub	purple/white	Feb
D. odora	ever. shrub	white/pink	Feb
Erica *arborea* var. *arborea*	ever. shrub	white	Mar–Apr
E. lusitanica	ever. shrub	pinkish white	Feb–Mar
Hamamelis × *intermedia*	decid. shrub	yellow, orange, red	Dec–Mar
H. japonica	decid. shrub	yellow	Jan–Feb
H. macrophylla	decid. shrub	yellow	Oct–Dec
H. mollis	decid. shrub	yellow	Jan–Feb
H. vernalis	decid. shrub	yellow-orange	Mar
H. virginiana	decid. shrub	yellow	Oct–Dec
Helleborus *foetidus*	ever. perennial	green	Feb–Apr
Lonicera *fragrantissima*	decid. shrub	white	Dec–Mar
L. × purpusii	decid. shrub	white	Dec–Mar
L. standishii	decid. shrub	white	Dec–Mar
Mahonia *japonica*	ever. shrub	yellow	Jan–Mar
M. × media 'Charity'	ever. shrub	yellow	Jan–Mar
Prunus *mume*	decid. tree	pink	Mar
Sarcococca *confusa*	ever. shrub	white	Jan–Feb
S. hookeriana var. digyna	ever. shrub	white	Jan–Feb
S. hookeriana var. humilis	ever. shrub	white	Jan–Feb
S. orientalis	ever. shrub	white	Jan–Feb
S. ruscifolia	ever. shrub	white	Jan–Feb
Skimmia *japonica* 'Rubella'	ever. shrub	red buds to white flowers	Nov–Apr

Plant Name	Plant Type	Color	Season of Interest
Viburnum × *bodnantense* 'Dawn'	decid. shrub	pink	Jan–Mar
V. farreri	decid. shrub	pink	Jan–Mar
V. farreri 'Nanum'	decid. shrub	pink	Jan–Mar
V. grandiflorum	decid. shrub	white	Jan–Mar

Public Winter Gardens

Although most fine public gardens of the Northwestern United States do not have designated winter gardens, they integrate into their collections many plants that provide interest in the depth of winter.

BRITISH COLUMBIA

Vancouver
Queen Elizabeth Park
Winter Garden, University of British Columbia
Botanical Garden
VanDusen Botanical Garden

Victoria
Beacon Hill Park
Butchart Gardens
Winter Garden, Horticulture Centre of the Pacific

CALIFORNIA

Mendocino
Mendocino Coast Botanical Gardens

OREGON

Eugene
Hendricks Park Rhododendron Garden
University of Oregon campus

Portland
Berry Botanic Garden
Elk Rock, the Garden of the Bishop's
Close Winter Garden, Hoyt Arboretum
Leach Botanical Garden

WASHINGTON

Bainbridge Island
The Bloedel Reserve

Federal Way
Rhododendron Species Foundation Display Gardens

Kingston
Heronswood, the author's garden, is open to the public
twice each year. For dates, call (206) 297-4172.

Seattle
Carl S. English, Jr. Botanical Gardens
(Hiram M. Chittenden Locks)
Children's Hospital & Medical Center grounds
Joseph A. Witt Winter Garden,
Washington Park Arboretum
Parsons Gardens
University of Washington campus
University of Washington Center for
Urban Horticulture
Volunteer Park
Woodland Park Zoological Gardens

Tacoma
Point Defiance Park

Woodinville
Chateau Ste. Michelle Winery grounds

Plant Buying Directory

The maritime Northwest abounds in high-quality retail nurseries where you can find many of the plants mentioned in this book. Harder-to-find species often can be located through mail-order nurseries across the United States, and by visiting the many annual plant sales offered in spring and autumn. Listed below are some reliable mail-order nurseries that sell plants that provide winter interest for Northwest gardens. All plants mentioned in the book are available from Heronswood Nursery. Inquire about current catalog price when corresponding with each source.

ANDRE VIETTE FARM AND NURSERY
Route 1, PO Box 16, Fishersville, VA 22939

CAMELLIA FOREST NURSERY
PO Box 291, Chapel Hill, NC 27514

COLLECTOR'S NURSERY
1602 NE 162nd Avenue, Vancouver, WA 98684

COLVOS CREEK NURSERY
PO Box 1512, Vashon Island, WA 98070

EASTERN PLANT SPECIALTIES
PO Box 226, Georgetown Island, ME 04548

FORESTFARM
990 Tetherow Road, Williams, OR 97544

GOSSLER FARMS NURSERY
1200 Weaver Road, Springfield, OR 97477

GREER GARDENS
1280 Goodpasture Island Road, Eugene, OR 97401

HERONSWOOD NURSERY
7530 288th Street NE, Kingston, WA 98346

HOLBROOK FARM AND NURSERY
115 Lance Road, PO Box 368, Fletcher, NC 28732

KURT BLUEMEL, INC.
2543 Hess Road, Fallston, MD 21047

LAMB NURSERIES
East 101 Sharp Avenue, Spokane, WA 99202

SISKIYOU RARE PLANT NURSERY
2825 Cummings Road, Medford, OR 97501

WASHINGTON EVERGREEN NURSERY
PO Box 388, Brooks Branch Road, Leicester, NC 28748

WE-DU NURSERY
Route 5, PO Box 724, Marion, NC 28752

WOODLANDER'S NURSERY
1128 Colleton Avenue, Aiken, SC 29801

Bibliography

Bean, W. J. TREES AND SHRUBS HARDY IN THE BRITISH ISLES, Volumes I–V. London: St. Martin's Press, 1980.

Coats, Alice M. GARDEN SHRUBS AND THEIR HISTORIES. New York: Simon & Schuster, 1992.

Hillier Nurseries. THE HILLIER MANUAL OF TREES AND SHRUBS, 6th ed. Great Britain: Redwood Press Ltd., 1992.

Lacy, Allen. THE GARDEN IN AUTUMN. New York: Atlantic Monthly Press, 1990.

Lancaster, Roy. SHRUBS THROUGH THE SEASONS. London: Harper-Collins, 1991.

Lawrence, Elizabeth L. GARDENS IN WINTER. New York: Harper-Collins, 1961.

Oakley, Myrna. PUBLIC AND PRIVATE GARDENS OF THE NORTHWEST. Wilsonville, OR: Beautiful America Publishing Company, 1990.

Phillips, Roger, and Martyn Rix. SHRUBS. New York: Random House, 1989.

Rice, Graham, and Elizabeth Strangman. THE GARDENER'S GUIDE TO GROWING HELLEBORES. Portland, OR: Timber Press, 1993.

Verey, Rosemary. THE GARDEN IN WINTER. New York: Little, Brown, 1988.

Whitner, Jan Kowalczewski. GARDEN TOURING IN THE PACIFIC NORTHWEST: A GUIDE TO GARDENS AND SPECIALTY NURSERIES IN OREGON, WASHINGTON, AND BRITISH COLUMBIA. Edmonds, WA: Alaska Northwest Books, 1993.

More Reading

You can obtain a free selected list of the most current books on winter and fall gardening, compiled by Valerie Easton, librarian, Elisabeth C. Miller Library, University of Washington Center for Urban Horticulture. Send a stamped, self-addressed legal-sized (#10) envelope to **Cascadia Gardening Series, Sasquatch Books, 1008 Western Avenue, Suite 300, Seattle, WA 98104.**

Index

(Bold numbers refer to material in the plant characteristics tables in the appendix.)

A–B

Abeliophyllum distichum,
  37–38, **82**
Abies procera, 23, **78**
Acanthus mollis, 66
Acer, 10–12, **74**
  A. davidii, 10
  A. griseum, 11–12, 56
  A. pensylvanicum, 11
  A. rufinerve, 10–11
  A. tegmentosum, 11
Acidic soil, 6
Amendments, organic,
  5–6
Apricot, 50–51
Arbutus, 12, **74**
  A. × andrachnoides, 12
  A. menziesii, 12
Arctostaphylos,
  12–13, **74**
  A. canescens, 13
  A. columbiana, 13
  A. manzanita, 13
  A. uva-ursi, 12–13
Autumn planting, 7
Azara microphylla,
  38, **82**
Barberry, 26–27,
  38–39, 62–63
Bare-root trees,
  planting, 7, 8
Beautyberry, 63–64

Berberis, 26–27, 38–39,
  49, 62–63, **78**, **88**
  B. calliantha, 27
  B. darwinii, 38–39
  B. gladwynensis, 27
  B. jamesiana, 63
  B. julianae, 26–27
  B. linearifolia, 39
  B. parvifolia, 62
  B. × stenophylla, 26
  B. wilsoniae, 63
Bergenia cordifolia, **78**
Berries, 62–72, **88**
Betula, 13–14, **74**
  B. albo-sinensis var.
    septentrionalis, 13
  B. apoiensis, 14
  B. jacquemontii, 14
  B. nana, 14
  B. nigra, 14
Birch, 13–14
Black lily turf, 31
Box-leaf azara, 38
Bulbs, 37, 58

C

Callicarpa, 28,
  63–64, **88**
  C. bodinieri var.
    giraldii, 63
  C. dichotoma, 63

C. japonica, 63
  C. mollis, 63
Calluna, 69
Camellia, 39–40, 50, **92**
  C. japonica, 40
  C. oleifera, 39–40
  C. saluensis, 40
  C. sasanqua, 40
  C. sinensis, 39
  C. × williamsii, 40
Castanopsis chrysophylla,
  34, **78**
Ceanothus, 13
Cedrus atlantica, 23, **78**
Celastrus, 33
Chamaecyparis, **78**
  C. lawsoniana,
    23–24, 71
  C. obtusa, 24, 65
Cherry, 50–51
Chimonanthus, **82**, **92**
  C. praecox, 41
  C. praecox var.
    luteus, 41
Chionodoxa, 42, 59, **82**
Cistus, 12, 13
Clay soil, 5
Clematis, 41, 48,
  61, **82**, **92**
  C. armandii, 61
  C. cirrhosa, 61
Color, 4

Conifers, 22–26
Cornus, 14, 15–16,
  48, 49, **74**
  C. alba, 15
  C. kousa, 15
  C. stolonifera, 15
Corylopsis, 41–42,
  48, 55, 57, **82**
  C. glabrescens, 41–42
  C. pauciflora, 41,
    52, 60
  C. sinensis, 14, 41
  C. spicata, 41
Corylus avellana, 16, **74**
Cotinus, 13
Cotoneaster, 64–65, **88**
  C. bullatus, 64
  C. 'Cornubia', 64
  C. horizontalis, 88
  C. × 'Hybridus
    Pendulus', 64–65
  C. lacteus, 64
  C. × 'Rothschildianus',
    65
Crape myrtle, 17
Crocus, 59
Cryptomeria japonica,
  24, 65, **78**
Cultivation, 5–9
Cupressus glabra, 24, **78**
Cyclamen, 58–59, **82**
  C. coum, 58, 59
  C. hederifolium, 58
  C. persicum, 58

D–E

Daphne, 42–43, **82, 92**
  D. blagayana, 42–43
  D. laureola, 42–43
  D. laureola var.
    philippi, 42
  D. mezereum, 42–43
  D. odora, 42–43
Dawn redwood, 17–18

Design, 1–4
Deutzia, 40
Disanthus cercidifolius, 14
Disease, 9
Dogwood, 15–16
Drought, 8
Elaeagnus, 27–28, **78**
  E. × ebbiginii 'Gilt
    Edge', 27–28, 64
  E. pungens, 27
Epimedium, 34, 61
Eranthis hyemalis, 59
Erica, 43–44, 69, **82, 92**
  E. arborea var.
    arborea, 44
  E. carnea, 44
  E. × darleyensis, 43
  E. lusitanica, 44
Euonymus, 33, 65, **88**
  E. europaeus, 65
Euphorbia amygdaloides
  var. robbiae, 28,
  54, 61, 68, **78**
Eurya japonica,
  28–29, **78**
Evergreen trees, broad-
  leaved, 26–36

F–H

Feeding See Fertilizer,
  Organic amendments
Fertilizer, 5, 8
Firethorn, 69–70
Flowers, 37–61, **82**
Foliage, 22–36, **78**
Forsythia, 40
Fragrance, 3, **92–93**
Full shade, defined, 7
Full sun, defined, 7
Galanthus, 37
Garrya, 44–45, **84**
  G. elliptica, 44–45
  G. fremontii, 45
  G. × issaquahensis, 45

Gaultheria, 69
  G. procumbens, 43
Gladwyn iris, 68
Gooseberry, 53–54
Hacquetia epipactis,
  59, **84**
Hamamelis, 45–46,
  57, **84, 92**
  H. × intermedia, 46
  H. japonica, 45
  H. mollis, 45
Harry Lauder's
  walking stick, 16
Heath, 43–44
Hellebore, 46–48
Helleborus, 46–48,
  57, **84, 92**
  H. argutifolius,
    46–47, 53
  H. foetidus, 47
  H. niger, 47
  H. × orientalis, 47
Helianthemum, 12
Holly, 29–30, 66–67
Honeysuckle, 49, 72
Hydrangea, 40

I–K

Idesia polycarpa, 66, **88**
Ilex, 29–30, 66–67,
  78, 90
  I. aquifolium, 29, 66
  I. crenata, 29–30, 67
  I. pedunculosa, 66
  I. 'September Gem',
    67
  I. verticillata, 18, 67
Insects, 9
Integrated pest
  management, 9
Iris, 59–60, **84, 88**
  I. foetidissima, 68
  I. unguicularis, 59

Irrigation, 8
Itea, 40
Jasminum nudiflorum,
  48, **84**
Juniperus, **78**
  J. chinensis, 65
  J. squamata, 24–25
Kinnikinnick, 12

L

Lagerstroemia, 17
Lamiastrum, 55
Lamium, 55, **78**
  L. maculatum, 30
Landscaping *See* Design
Lathyrus vernus,
  42, 60, **84**
Lavandula, 13
Leucothoe, **78**
  L. davisae, 30–31
  L. fontanesiana, 30–31
Lindera obtusiloba,
  48–49, **84**
Location, planting, 6–7
Lonicera, 49, 72,
  84, 90, 92
  L. alesuosmoides, 72
  L. fragrantissima, 49
  L. henryi, 72
  L. nitida, 67
  L. × purpusii, 49
  L. standishii, 49

M–O

Madrona, 12
Mahonia, 49–50,
  55, 57, **84, 92**
  *M. × 'Arthur
    Menzies'*, 50
  M. bealei, 50
  M. lomariifolia, 50
  M. × media, 50
Manzanita, 12–13

Maple, 10–12
*Metasequoia
  glyptostroboides*,
  17–18, **76**
Microbiota decussata,
  25, **78**
Millium effusim, 59
Miss Robb's spurge, 28
Mountain ash, 70–71
Nandina domestica, **80**
Nitrogen, 5
Oak, 34–35
Omphalodes, 60, **84**
  O. cappadocica, 60
  O. verna, 60
Ophiogon, **80**
  O. planiscapus, 38
  O. planiscapus
    'Nigrescens', 31, 48
Organic amendments,
  5–6
Organic matter, 5
Osmanthus, 31–32, **80**
  O. × burkwoodii, 32
  O. decorus, 32
  O. delavayi, 32
  O. heterophyllus,
    31–32
Osmarea × burkwoodii,
  32

P

Pachistima, 33–34, **80**
  P. canbyi, 33
  P. myrsinites, 33
Pachysandra, **80**
  P. terminalis, 33
  P. Vancouveria, 34
Parochetus communis,
  60, **84**
Parrotia persica, 18, **76**
Partial shade, defined, 7
Perennials,
  26–36, 58–61

Pernettya mucronata,
  68–69, **90**
Persea, **76**
  P. ichangense, 18–19
  P. yunnanensis, 18–19
Persian ironwood, 18
Pesticides, 9
Pests, 9
Philadelphus, 40
Picea, **80**
  P. omorika, 25
  P. orientalis, 25, 71
Pine, 19
Pinus, 19, **76**
  P. bungeana, 19
  P. densiflora, 19
  P. sylvestris, 25
Placement, plant, 2–4
Planning *See* Design
Plant placement, 2–4
Plant selection, 1–4
Planting, 7–8
Planting location, 6–7
Planting times, 7
Polymers, 6
Primula veris, 48
Pruning, 9
Prunus, 50–51, **86**
  P. mume, 51
  P. subhirtella, 50–51
Pseudocydonia sinensis,
  19–20, **76**
Pulmonaria,
  42, 55, 60–61, **86**
  P. angustifolia, 60
  P. rubra, 60
  P. saccharata, 60
Pyracantha,
  64, 69–70, **90**
  P. angustifolia, 69
  P. atalantioides
    'Gnome', 69
  P. coccinea 'Lalandei',
    69
  P. 'Teton', 69

Q–R

Quercus, 34–35, **80**
Q. glauca, 34
Q. hypoleucoides, 34
Q. ilex, 34
Q. myrsinifolia, 34
Q. suber, 34
Rhododendron,
51–53, 69, **86**
R. bureavii, 52
R. ciliatum, 52
R. dauricum, 51
R. moupinense, 52
R. mucronulatum,
42, 48, 51
R. 'Olive', 52–53
R. 'Praecox', 51–52
R. strigillosum, 52
R. yakushimanum, 52
Rhus, 13
Ribes, 53–54, **86**
R. laurifolium, 53
R. sanguineum, 53
Rubus
R. cockburnianus, 19
R. tricolor, 54

S

Salix, 20–21, **76**
S. alba, 20
S. alba var. vitellina, 20
S. chaenomeloides, 20
S. daphnoides, 20
S. gracilistyla, 20
S. melanostachys, 20
S. purpurea, 16, 20
Sandy soil, 5
Santolina, 13
Sarcococca,
30, 54–55, **86, 92**
S. confusa, 54
S. hookeriana var.
digyna, 54

S. hookeriana var.
humilis, 54
S. orientalis, 54
S. ruscifolia, 50, 54
Scent See Fragrance
Selection, plant, 1–4
Shade, full, 7
Shade, partial, 7
Shrubs, 10–21, 26–36,
37–57, 62–72
Silverberry, 27–28
Site analysis, 2
Skimmia japonica,
55, **86, 92**
Soil, 5–6
Sorbus, 70–71, **90**
S. aucuparia, 70
S. forrestii, 70
S. hupehensis, 70
S. prattii, 70
Spindletree, 65
Spiraea × bumalda, 39
Spring planting, 7
Spring vetchling, 60
Stachyurus,
48, 55–56, **86**
S. chinensis, 55
S. praecox,
12, 40, 53, 55–56
Stewartia, 21, 49, **76**
S. koreana, 21
S. monodelpha, 21
S. pseudocamellia, 21
Stranvaesia,
64, 71–72, **80, 90**
S. davidiana, 71
S. davidiana var.
undulata, 71
Styrax, 49
Sun, full, 7
Sycoparrotia, 56–57, **86**
S. semidecidua, 56, **86**
Sycopsis, 56–57, **86**
S. sinensis, 56

T–Z

Taxus baccata, 25, **80**
Thuja plicata, 26, **80**
Topsoil, 6
Trachycarpus fortunei, 66
Trees, 10–21,
37–57, 62–72
Tropaeolum speciosum,
41
Tsuga
T. canadensis, 63
T. heterophylla, 46
Vaccinium ovatum, 33
Vancouveria, 61, **80**
V. planipetala, 27
Viburnum, 35–36,
57, **80, 88, 92**
V. awabuki var.
chindo, 35
V. × bodnantense, 57
V. cinnamomifolium,
35
V. davidii, 35
V. farreri, 57
V. grandiflorum, 57
V. × pragense, 35
V. rhytidophyllum, 35
Vines, 61, 72
Waldsteinia ternata, 38
Watering, 8
Weigela, 40
White forsythia, 37–38
White Nancy, 30
Willow, 20–21
Winter hazel, 41–42
Winter-blooming
jasmine, 48
Wintersweet, 41
Witch hazel, 45–46
Yucca, 13